HORIZON READERS

# ON THE TRAIL
PAGES FROM THE WRITINGS OF
## GREY OWL

Edited by

## E. E. REYNOLDS

ILLUSTRATED BY STUART TRESILIAN

CAMBRIDGE
AT THE UNIVERSITY PRESS
1940

CAMBRIDGE UNIVERSITY PRESS
Cambridge, New York, Melbourne, Madrid, Cape Town,
Singapore, São Paulo, Delhi, Tokyo, Mexico City

Cambridge University Press
The Edinburgh Building, Cambridge CB2 8RU, UK

Published in the United States of America by
Cambridge University Press, New York

www.cambridge.org
Information on this title: www.cambridge.org/9781107600157

© Cambridge University Press 1940

First published 1940
First paperback edition 2011

*A catalogue record for this publication is available from the British Library*

ISBN 978-1-107-60015-7 Paperback

*Grey Owl*

# Who was Grey Owl?

PEOPLE still argue as to whether Grey Owl was really an Indian by birth or only by adoption. What is certain is that about 1905 he began work as a canoeman and voyageur on the rivers and in the vast forests of Canada. For a time he lived with a band of Ojibway Indians on an island in Lake Temagami. He quickly learned their language and became so much one of them that they adopted him. They gave him the name of Wa-Sha-Quon-Asin, which means, 'He who walks by night', for they noticed how fond he was of travelling after sunset. That Ojibway name has been translated into English as GREY OWL.

He soon became known as an expert woodsman and trapper; he showed a reckless courage in face of the many dangers and emergencies that meet the traveller in that wild country; he came to know the ways of rivers, of rapids, and of the animals of the forests.

Then came the outbreak of war in 1914. He enlisted under the name of Archie Belaney, and for three years fought in France as a sniper. He was wounded and gassed, and at the end of 1917 was discharged and sent back to Canada. The lameness from his wound, and his weakened health, made it impossible for him to follow his old strenuous life, so he turned to trapping.

It was not long before a change came over him. Perhaps as a result of all the suffering he had seen in France, he began to feel sorry for the animals he trapped, and at length he decided to give up an occupation which meant so much cruelty. For a time he suffered greatly; his small army pension was not enough to live on, so he began to write down accounts of his experiences.

He recalled the old times on the rivers as a canoeman, and the risks and dangers of the trail. Then he set down what he knew of the Indians and their way of living, and next he wrote of some new friends he had made—the Beavers. He had found his mission. He would try to make people kinder to animals; he would do all he could to preserve the great forests of Canada, and lastly he would try to save the remnants of the race that had adopted him.

He wrote four books: *The Men of the Last Frontier*, which tells of the old days as a voyageur; *Tales of an Empty Cabin*, in which he records many of his adventures in the woods; *Pilgrims of the Wild*, which is an autobiography containing an account of how he came to protect the beavers; and, *The Adventures of Sajo and Her Beaver People*, a story of two young Indians and two beavers.

These books made him famous throughout the world. The Canadian Government employed him to guard the wild life round Lake Ajawaan in the Prince Albert National Park, and there he had that wonderful log-cabin which he shared with Jelly Roll, Rawhide, and their family.

He came to England to lecture about his animal friends, and then went on to the United States to speak his message there; his last lecture was given in his own country early in 1938. Then he returned to his cabin and the lake with its forest—and the beavers who were then still sleeping their winter sleep.

Worn out with his long months of constant travel and lecturing, he had no strength to resist illness, and after a short time in hospital, he died on the 13th of April, 1938. They buried him by the shores of his lake where the animals had learned to know him as their friend.

# CONTENTS

## CHAPTER ONE

## *The River Trail*

IF you are staunch of heart and strong in small adversities, and can face the sun and wind; if you would like to try sleeping in a tent on a bed of fragrant balsam brush, and sitting on the ground to eat, and if, above all, you have an abounding sense of humour, we'll take a voyage down this so impetuously autocratic river, you and I.

\*    \*    \*    \*    \*    \*

That night we sleep in the tent allotted to us, and just after we have got nicely to sleep, someone slaps smartly on the canvas door and shouts in a loud, unsympathetic voice, 'Shake a leg there! Daylight in the swamp!' A muffled grumbling from one of the other occupants of the tent asks, 'What the heck time is it?' 'What do you care what time it is?' comes back this inexorable voice. 'It's away after three o'clock. Going to stay in bed all your life? Get after your canoes'—Boyd Mathewson, brigade chief, at his best. Red Landreville, who is in our tent, suggests that the canoes must be awful wild when a person can't wait for daylight to catch them but has to creep up on them under cover of the darkness. And certainly the daylight *does* look a little thin.

Those hard-driving, pitiless chiefs! How we hated
them, loved them, thumbed our noses at them (meta-
phorically speaking, or if otherwise, most discreetly
from well-selected cover), and broke our backs to
fulfil, and sometimes exceed, their orders. How we
bragged of having worked for them and boasted over
our 'miles a day' and 'pounds a trip' on a portage.

But we are not here to boast; there's a two hundred
and fifty mile journey to be made after breakfast, and
we are going to see some speed. No, brother, we are
not going to do it all to-day, nor even this week. This
is more or less of a pleasure trip, thirty miles a day, or
forty at the most—what'll we do the rest of the day?
Say, you're quite a humorist too, ain't you—you'll
get along, I guess.

Breakfast is soon over, and canoes are loaded and
trimmed. There is the minimum of bustle, and no confusion whatsoever, as loads have been assembled and
lashed the night before and there is nothing to do but
pack the grub-boxes, one for each canoe, two men to a
canoe. The only fanfare that heralds the starting out
of one of these expeditions, some of which last six
months, is the laconic 'Well, boys, let's go' of the chief.

And go we do. Paddles dip in unison, backs bend
and sway, canoes leap forward at the rate of four miles
to the hour. The great sun rises, goes on up, getting
smaller but hotter as it goes, and becomes a burning
red ball that beats down on unprotected heads and
hands and faces. As the day advances the air becomes

more torrid; the lakes lie like seas of molten glass, and the palpitating landscape is immersed in a screeching, scorching glare. High overhead in a metallic sky the sun, like a burnished copper gong, beats a fierce tattoo to which the whole face of Nature quivers, and to whose tune the rows of jack-pines topping the distant ridges writhe, and swing, and sway in the steps of a fantastic sun-dance, reeling drunkenly in the shimmering waves of a merciless, breathless heat. But we don't let a little warm weather bother us; this is August, and the hot weather is about over in this North-country. The odd hot day gives the boys a break—sweats some of the infernal laziness out of their hides, says Charlie Dougal—resting softens a man——!

So, speed, speed, speed, grip the canoe ribs with your knees, drive those paddles deep, throw your weight on to them, click them on those gunnels twenty-five strokes to the minute; spurn that water in gurgling eddies behind you, bend those backs, and drive! Sternsmen, keep your eyes on the far objective, far off in the blue distance, and take your proper allowance for a side-wind, don't make leeway like a greenhorn! Thus, eyes fixed ahead, watchful of everything, breath coming deeply, evenly, backs swinging freely from the hips, paddles dipping and flashing, we drive her—fifty miles a day or bust. Some have busted, but not this outfit. You thought you heard me say thirty miles a day? Perhaps you did, but Dougal is running this brigade, not me. We are to make the first hundred miles in

two days, he says, which is sense; we want to get out
of the lake country while we have a fair wind to help
us; the Indians say the wind is going to change, and
so slow us up.

A duck flies in before the canoes, and taking the
water, flaps along in front of us as though hurt. She
has young ones hidden somewhere and is trying to
decoy us away from them by this offer of easy capture,
keeping just far enough ahead to be out of reach. Her
ruse succeeds quite well, because we don't want her
brood in the first place, and we are not going their way
anyhow. She continues this pretence of disability until
we nearly catch up to her, when she suddenly recovers,
flies a short piece ahead, and commences the performance all over again. She does this time and time
again, with a maddening persistence and an unnecessary expenditure of energy that, in this heat, makes us
burst out into renewed streams of perspiration just to
look at her—and all for nothing. We are just beginning to regard her with the greatest repugnance
when, having lured us, as she supposes, to a safe distance, she flies back home, pursued by the objurgations
of the entire brigade; except the Indians, who show
no emotion whatsoever and pass no comment, though
they watch the duck's every move intently, as they do
everything else that is seen.

On the portages the leaves hang limp and listless,
and the still air is acrid with the resinous odour of
boiling spruce gum. Here men sweat under enormous

burdens; earlier in the Summer, clouds of mosquitoes
and black-flies would envelope them in biting swarms.
But it is August, and the fly season is over, and those
that are left are too weak to do any damage, and sit
balefully regarding us from nearby limbs of trees.
Pattering of moccasined feet on the narrow trail, as
men trot with the canoes, one to a man, or step easily
along under their loads; and in a miraculously short
space of time everything is over to the far side. Canoes
are re-loaded expertly, and we are away again. But
out on the lake there is a change. A welcome breeze
fans us, cooling us off, while it dries the sweat—also
our throats. Someone commences to sing in a high,
thin tenor, this seeming to be just the right note for a
desiccated throat; the refrain is, aptly enough, 'How
dry I am——'. We all laugh and join in the chorus.
We begin to enjoy ourselves, to rejoice in the fluid
rhythm of the canoes, to feel the ecstasy of this wild,
free, vigorous life that seems all at once to be the only
life worth living. The free wind of the open has by now
blown away a thousand petty thoughts of profit, or of
desire to prevail over someone, or of device or stratagem
whereby to gain preferment. For this is not a life of
dodge and subterfuge, save only where necessary to
gain, not what another may have possession of, but
only what Nature offers for the means to live, to
carry on.

And we carry on; there is no let-up. Any faltering
will draw meaning looks, and perhaps meaninger

remarks from our decidedly humorous, but quite re-
morseless and entirely inflexible chiefs—Blood-for-
Breakfast and Quick-Lunch Dougal and their piratical
crew are headed for the River, men obsessed by the
purpose of covering Distance, disciples of speed, knight-
errants of the canoe, devotees of the Trail. And we
must needs follow; you must stay with it, my friend.
Here is where the rich man's riches buy him nothing,
and where a parading of his business acumen will
only get him in wrong with his guides. And it is no
use audibly admiring the scenery (not unless you are
doing your share, however little it may be), because
you can't curry favour with the landscape. This,
Mister, is the real thing, and no moving-picture set.
You are asking me why all the hurry, and where *is*
this so-famous Mississauga River? Well, it is just
seventy-five miles in from town, including sixteen
portages. No, sir, we are not trying to do it all in one
day, though it has been done. This is to be an easy trip,
on account of our guest, that's you, and we will con-
sume all of a day and a half. You decide that further
speech seems unnecessary, futile, in face of the facts.

And so, in a continuous alternation of lake and
portage, dazzling sea of glare and oven-like, leafy
tunnel, we go on. When do we eat? thinks you—or do
we eat? You begin to wonder. But, sooner or later,
noon comes and we prepare a much needed meal. The
cooking is not complicated. There is only one precept
to abide by, so Augustus, the financier, informs us, and

that is to put salt into everything except tea and jam; that way, he says, you can't go wrong. But we soon find that this Gus fellow is also something of a humorist, because there is no jam, and nobody ever puts salt in tea. So the matter becomes quite simple. On talking the matter over with this financial expert, we are told that it is not good economy to carry stuff you don't need; it doesn't pay. But he has a great nose for his own advantage, and being German, is well provided with *urbswurst*, and with it he makes a very palatable soup, which he shares around.

Gus's pleasantry concerning the non-existent jam brings up the subject of provisions. Limited to a canoe-load of supplies for each two men for five months —the duration of some of these trips—and with no trading posts, in this area, at which to replenish, the provision list is shorn of all luxuries and frills. And although this is more or less of a light trip, the dictates of established custom are adhered to, so we have not only no jam (because it has an uncomfortable fashion of coming open and mixing with the soap and matches), but also no potatoes, eggs, caviare, nor canned lobster. The last two items are entirely legendary in character so far as we are concerned, and we do not miss them. But we have flour, salt and baking powder with which to make bannock, a kind of large scone cooked over hot coals; this delicacy is of Scotch origin, having been introduced by the Hudson Bay people who were largely Scotsmen. It is also known as Indian loaf. It

is going to be your principal article of diet, so take a
good look at one—yes, you are right, it makes no
attempt to float out of your hand; but don't drop it on
your foot; it doesn't bounce. It stays right with you.
We have long ago exploded the theory that ordinary
bread is the staff of life. We almost never eat it, and
have managed to thrive to quite a size without it. No
one wants to kill a large animal like a deer or moose,
and have the meat spoil; we have no time to spend
drying and smoking it as the Indians do. Instead we
bring along several sides of very salt pork which have
to be parboiled, in slices, before it can be fried and
eaten; it comes in large, corpse-like slabs that go under
the various titles of sow-belly, long clear, and rattle-
snake pork. The flavour indicates the last name as
being the most applicable. We have also tea, sugar,
white beans, which latter have a very high nutriment
value, a few dried apples, and soap, matches and
tobacco. This frugal but stimulating fare is eked out
with fresh fish, of which we have the very best and lots
of it, and also berries in season. The idea, of course,
is to get as much solid eating material for as little
weight and bulk as possible; hence the elimination of
potatoes and canned goods.

This list seems rather limited, you think. Well don't
say it aloud. These men, used to self-denial and hardship of all kinds, would think you were complaining.
Remember, reader, you are away back in the days of
the pork and bannock régime, when a man who

brought along milk or breakfast bacon was deemed to be lowering the standard of manhood. Butter was taboo, not only because we never even thought of it, but also because its unlucky owner caused delay and friction as he fussed around in his futile attempts to preserve it and keep it from turning to oil in temperatures of ninety or a hundred in the shade. A man who was found to be in clandestine possession of butter was considered to be lacking in force of character, and it was suspected that his morals were rancid. Goods labelled 'Canned roast beef' and 'Tinned dinner' were contemptuously referred to as 'Horse', and the libertine who was caught eating them was said to be digging his grave with his teeth. And this was not all mere caprice, as such things were heavy for their size, didn't last long, and took up a lot of room in a canoe that could have been put to better use, and when after a few weeks these whimsies had been consumed, the culprit had perforce to beg donations from the meagre supplies of his fellow travellers, so that one having these luxurious tastes was something in the nature of a menace to society, or a public enemy. To-day it would be impossible for me to live that way, and I fear, too, that my speed limit has been much reduced.

Eating, under ordinary circumstances, is merely a means of sustaining life, at least in our severely simple and unpolished social state. Yet after a long, hard siege at the paddle, the pole, or the tump-line, a meal

can become the sum total of the recreation, the
relaxation and the entertainment of the day, and be
an event of some importance; assuming under these
circumstances a dignity and significance out of all
proportion to the short time spent in cooking it, or the
fifteen minutes enjoyment that it gives. And then the
cool, lazy smoke in the shade afterwards; that is even
better. Stretched out beneath an umbrella-topped
jack-pine, his pipe going, contented, with that feeling
of satisfaction that comes of labour successfully ac-
complished and the thought of congenial labour yet
to do, quietly glorying in his strength and fitness and
proficiency, as much a part of his environment as the
tree he leans against, your true voyageur would trade
places with no king. There are different ideas of comfort; to some it consists in a feather bed, or in the
personal service given, for pay, by 'lesser' men; to us
it means getting outside of a full meal, or having our
feet dry, or, in fly season, having an hour's surcease
from the mosquitoes; or, greatest of all, in experiencing
the unutterable sense of relief, the feeling of luxurious
ease that possesses a man's soul when he puts down a
burden after carrying it, maybe, up three hills, or for
a long distance on the uncertain footing provided by
a lot of loosely-fitting boulders that move and wobble
at every step. There's nothing just like it.

The dinner hour doesn't last long; it isn't even an
hour before we are ready to go again. Fires are carefully put out, for the menace of forest fire hangs con-

stantly over us, an ever-present threat. Quickly we
resume our paddles and are away again. In the
interim the sun has moved and, having been well
burned on one side, we are now to be nicely browned
on the other. This is no relief of course, but is at least
a change; and after all there is something to be said
for symmetry. We pass over a series of small, still
lakes, where the arabesque tracery of the foliage is
reflected as in a looking-glass. We pass historic places,
thick with legend and tradition; the remains of an
ancient Hudson's Bay post, relict of an older, wilder
day. Its timbers can still be seen, and on the knoll
behind it is a primitive Indian graveyard; we pass the
Place-of-Crying-Mink, where sometimes is heard the
desolate, awful wailing of a phantom mink; to the
South lies Woman Portage where a woman long dead
walks at the full of the moon. There is a camping
ground shunned by the Indians, because a ghost
beaver who lived nearby once stole a hunter's paddles,
and with very unghostly perspicacity cut them up and
thoughtfully hid the pieces. This left the hunter
stranded until he had made new paddles, upon which
he immediately left the country. A steep bank is
pointed out, where the May-May-Gwense, Indian
elves, slide up and down in the moonlight for amuse-
ment. Some claim to have watched them and if you
don't believe it, there is the little trail, plain to be seen.
Back in the hills hereabouts, there is known to have
been found, by an Indian named The Cat, an enor-

mous footprint of a man. It is said to have been that
of an Iroquois, one of those warriors who ravaged this
country about a century ago, and are remembered by
one or two still living; he is still supposed to be lurking
in the vicinity.

In a narrow strait that joins two lakes, we meet an
old prospector; he has an Indian guide, because he is
not a water dog, as a canoeman is termed, but a desert
rat from Nevada, and therefore has no knowledge of
water travel. The Indian says that this desert man
carries a water-flask everywhere he goes—in a country
that is more than half water—and fills all available
vessels with water before going to bed at night. Conversation reveals that he knows his rocks very well
indeed; but everything else here is new to him. He has
noted our speed, and does not approve. He is never
in a hurry, he tells us. His theory is, that life is short
and we'll be a long time dead; so what's all the fury
about? We smile gently and tolerantly at this inex-
plicable foible of an old man, and wishing him lucky
prospecting with a wild halloo, which he answers with
a Piute war-whoop for a send-off, we race forward on
our way. We pass Indian camps where dogs that are
more than half wolf bark at us menacingly, and high
featured, tawny faces framed in lank black hair peer
out at us with eyes that are veiled, inscrutable, yet
strangely penetrating.

On the next portage we have our first mishap.
Baldy is carrying, defiantly, against expressed public
opinion, one of his outsize loads when the tump-line,

'*Baldy is carrying, defiantly, one of his outsize loads when the tump-line, an old one, breaks. The sudden release throws the little fellow forward on his face.*'

an old one, breaks. The sudden release throws the little fellow forward on his face, and his nose is bleeding. Self-conscious as usual, he sets out to explain. 'My tump-line was no good; they don't make 'em that way any more. A good man can't get the stuff to work with any more'. He goes on to say, with the blood dripping from his chin, that the world in general is hell-bound; even the mosquitoes are not what they were. Charlie (Quick-lunch) Dougal agrees, with heavy sarcasm, that the fly crop was a black failure this year; Red Landreville says yes, it's only too true, even gangsters don't use machine-guns these days—they are reduced to carrying concealed razor blades; it's a tough world. Zepherin, arriving on the scene, is in one of his Pistolian moods, and affecting to misunderstand the state of affairs, roars at the gore-stained Baldy, 'Ha! Me blood-stained bucko! Fightin', eh? And you with the best man in the world at your heels —you vampire! you ravaging scorpion, you!—you hideous monster, to be consortin' with decent men—' while Baldy stands in the silent dignity of forbearance and asserts, very obviously, that he is no monster, hasn't fought and doesn't want to fight, and only needs a new tump-line. This is forthcoming, with advice not to let it (the tump-line) get him down, and not to carry *all* the load at once as there is another day to-morrow, reminding him that there is too much rock here to bury a man decently, and that a corpse won't keep in this weather, and so forth.

Soon after this, at an improvised landing of logs, someone, picking up a canoe by the centre (the proper way), knocks Matogense, usually so sure-footed, over into the quaking bog the timbers are supposed to bridge, out of which he presently scrambles, covered with an evil-smelling coating of slime. Everybody at once remembers, inconveniently for Matogense, the story of his daughter who was fed the live fish to help her learn to swim, and it is suggested that he be given a bull-frog to eat so that he will be able to get around better in the mud. It is characteristic that his load, which he has fallen in with, is salvaged first while he is left to shift for himself, the argument being that he can crawl out and the provisions can not; and it is the consensus of opinion that a man has to be dragged in the mud a couple of times before he is worth a damn, anyway. But these are two mishaps too many. Men are getting tired; their movements are not so sure. Things are slowing up, and it is getting late. So it is to our intense relief that Aleck L'Espagnol, with a glance at the rapidly darkening sky and the now rising mists, sagely suggests that we call it a day and make camp. Surprisingly, that devastating speed-fiend, Dougal, and the terse-spoken, adamantine Mathewson both agree; and in this they show the best of judgment, for Aleck is held in general esteem for his wisdom.

Camp is quickly made within an encircling grove of giant red-pines, whose crenelated columns, all ruddy

in the firelight, stand about the place like huge pillars
that support a roof so high above us as to be invisible,
reaching up to unknown heights into the blackness,
giving us the feeling that we are encamped in some
old, deserted temple. While all around us is the inter-
minable, unfathomable forest, whose denizens live
in impenetrable privacy, and in the dark recesses of
which a thousand shadows lie in ambush all the day,
awaiting only the coming of night to creep out and
slowly, silently invest the whole world of trees, and
rocks, and water, and the sleeping camp. But the
camp is not sleeping yet; bannock has to be made for
the next day's consumption, and other preparations
completed for the morrow's journey. Everything is
quickly disposed in its proper place, the whole camp a
standing model of neatness and well-contrived arrange-
ment.

And then comes that hour of rest and quiet con-
tentment, when there is no sound save the light crackle
of burning wood and the odd murmur of a voice, when
all the face of Nature is immersed in that brooding
calm that comes down like an invisible curtain with
the falling of night. Besides the central fire most
everyone has settled down to sit and smoke, or sit and
talk, or just to sit. Talk turns to earlier days, and of
men, great men, and mighty men, and men who were
remarkable, in times gone by. Any conversation
among a bunch of woodsmen will inevitably work its
way round to these biographical anecdotes, which

invariably take the form of reminiscences commencing with such introductions as 'I mind one time——', or 'In the early days——', or ''Way back in '05, I think it was——', and are given with a great wealth of detail. And it is to be noticed that these are all tributes; the mean, the trifling, and the base have been forgotten, and at any ill-advised mention of them, a sudden silence is apt to fall upon the group. We hear of Joe McLean, the Indian, who in a storm at night, the canoe swamped and no longer able to hold two men, shouted good-bye to the tourist he was guiding, and letting go of the canoe, disappeared into the darkness and was never seen again alive. Many are the tales of Billy Friday who, on a bet, carried six bags of flour, one hundred pounds in each, from the wharf on Temagami lake up to the station, a distance of a hundred yards, part of it up hill. We are told, too, of the famous Larry Frost, another Indian, who fought on one occasion with nine men at once, and trimmed them all.

Then there was Joe Seiderquist, the white trapper, who did everything in a big way, and undertook a friendly wrestling match with a half-tame bear. Towards the close of the second bout he bit the bear so badly that they had to be separated. 'He was', stated the narrator, 'a hearty man; you should have heard him eat!' Joe, we are informed, borrowed a dog team from Dan O'Connor, who was the Big Shot at Temagami in those days; he was known as the King of Temagami. Joe kept the dogs all Winter, and brought them back safe and sound. But when the dogs arrived back in town Dan didn't recognise them, not having had the dogs very long in the first place. So Joe, for a joke, told Dan that he had lost the original team through the ice, paid for them, and sold Dan's own team back to him at a nice profit. This same Dan O'Connor was a man of rare ability, and performed prodigies of pioneering in that North country in the face of almost insuperable difficulties, all of which he overcame. He owned some hotels at the tourist resort that sprang up by the lake after the railroad came through, and would employ almost any means by which to boost his beloved town of Temagami. His resourcefulness was proverbial, and if there was any possible way of getting a thing done, he would do it; as for instance, when an important railroad magnate wished to examine into the game possibilities of the region, with a view to establishing a tourist traffic. This would be valuable, and Dan wanted it. But this official required duck shooting for his patrons, and he was coming at the one time of year when there were no ducks, in the middle of Summer. Dan decided to supply the ducks. This wouldn't be cheating, as there were always plenty of them in the proper season. So Dan had a crate of ducks sent up from the distant city. On their arrival Dan had an Indian take them over behind an island opposite the hotel. The magnate also arrived in due course, and sitting with O'Connor on the veranda after supper, began to ask about ducks.

About that time the Indian sauntered up, and held a desultory conversation with O'Connor in Indian. This was according to plan. The Indian had a gun, and presently moved off with it and was seen paddling over to the island. 'Where's he going?' asked the magnate. 'Duck hunting', replied O'Connor. 'Do you suppose he will get any?' enquired the interested railroad man. 'Sure he will', asserted the invincible Dan. Presently there was a fusillade behind the island. Shortly afterwards the same Indian paddled across to the landing before the Hotel, and as he walked slowly by, this astonished official was treated, in a wilderness removed a hundred and fifty miles from any farm, to the astounding spectacle of a round dozen of common barnyard ducks, tastefully arranged upon a pole.

Dan was wont to boast that he had brought 'steamships to Temagami on snowshoes!' This was almost a statement of fact, as he had taken some Indians and broken a trail through the snow-bound bush and over frozen lakes forty miles to Ville Marie in the dead of Winter, on snowshoes of course, leading on his return journey a procession of teams, each bearing a component part of the first wood-burning steamboat that ever sailed on Lake Temagami. He it was who, greeting Lord Charles Beresford on the occasion of his visit to that country, remarked that it was a momentous occasion, the Lord of the British Navy meeting the Lord of Temagami—two Lords so to speak—'So he'd feel at home', said Dan afterwards.

And now the talk becomes desultory, dies down. The men retire, and soon all sound ceases. And the fire begins to burn low, and from it a thin, white, wavering column of smoke ascends, up into the pine-tops, far above. The night-mist from off the water hangs in wisps and mingles with the smoke; until the fire dies at last, and the waiting shadows take final and complete possession, once and for all.

\*　　\*　　\*　　\*　　\*　　\*

Morning comes early with Boyd Mathewson, and once he is up, it is quite impossible for anyone else to sleep. Men stagger stiffly from their tents, and we all have a touch of that stale dryness, that washed-out feeling that comes on the morning after a forced march of any kind. And there is to be another one to-day, lasting to noon when, if there are no accidents or adverse winds, we will have arrived at the Mississauga River. Dougal, having already had a quick and very sketchy breakfast, is stepping around, bright as a new dollar and as smart as a particularly aggressive cricket. To the others he is, of course, nothing but an infestation and is earning, by his disturbing activities, some black looks and very pointed and uncomplimentary comment, none of which he heeds. Besides the fire squats Boyd, glowering in caustic silence at the leisurely movements of the men; by the process of raising one eyebrow while heavily depressing the other, and holding a fork at a kind of expectant angle over a suggestively empty frying-pan, he managed to achieve an appearance of almost malignant preparedness. The men, meanwhile, pretend an elaborate and maddening indifference to all this and continue, speedily enough, with the work of breaking camp, chuckling among themselves. Red Landreville expresses himself, under his breath, as being by no means in love with these blood-for-breakfast ideas; but Zepherin, in a loud voice intended to be overheard, allows that for his part, he is glad somebody woke him up, as he had slept so hard he nearly broke his neck, that three in the morning is as good a time as any to get up, as it gave a man time to have an appetite for dinner, and that he liked long days because he could do more work. In fact, he liked work so well, he stated, that he could easily lie down and sleep beside it. A cold silence from the direction of the fire greeted these well-chosen remarks.

However, after a short time these minor and half-jocular irritations pass off, and everybody is soon busy around the fire with their cooking apparatus, one tea-pail and a frying-pan to every two men. Billy Mitchell, who is a pretty good cook and quite justly proud of it, has prepared what he calls 'community pancakes' for the entire crowd. This is by way of asking the whole bunch out to dinner, so to speak, and it is much appreciated, and as Billy sets them out, he says, 'These pancakes look pretty good, by gosh', which brings an immediate chorus of dissent—'They don't look any too good to me'; and 'What's so good about them, the colour?'; and 'Whatcha ma'em with, a shovel?' and

'Their looks won't help them; better take a good look at them, you're seein' them for the last time!' But very soon they are all gone, which is about the best compliment they could have got.

Tents are folded, canoes are loaded, and we are away again. Paddles dip and swing (no, they don't flash—there is no sun, and won't be for another two hours) and canoes shoot ahead. You seem to ache in every joint, stiff from yesterday's gruelling drive, and muscles feel like rusty springs; but soon you burst into a profuse perspiration, which cleanses and lubricates the machinery and releases the hidden forces of energy for the day. It is fine weather to-day again. We are lucky; and the wind is with us, too. There are few cabins back in here; everyone (we haven't met anyone yet) lives in tents and a log camp is only a place to keep a cache of provisions, or a good place to go into out of the rain; and as these shelters are very far apart, it sometimes rains between cabins.

What do we do then? Well, we can't do a thing about it, so we let it rain. An ordinary shower stops nobody, but there are often days when sheets of driving rain, the dull skies, the dripping trees, soggy moss and streaming rocks blend in a monotonous monochrome of grey; when it is wise to stop and put up tents where there is plenty of wood, light a huge fire and make as merry as possible under the circumstances, drying off before the cheerful blaze beneath a canopy of tarpaulins. Sometimes a sudden storm, which you saw coming, but took a gambler's chance that it would pass a few miles to the Westward, catches you unprepared, and under the scant shelter of a hastily overturned canoe, its one end reared above the ground to give you room, you sit for hours and shiver yourself warm until the rain stops. You don't as a rule take these chances when on the Trail, but you do when you are with Mathewson or Dougal. Let's hope it doesn't rain, says you. And you're right. The infrequent camps we encounter are, you notice, open and generally contain supplies; nothing is hidden. In this country, a man who conceals his cache or locks his camp is considered to be an outlander, and is looked on with suspicion as one who would steal— it seems to follow; and not till easy transportation brings in a few of the wrong kind of people is this unwritten law ever broken.

As we approach the head of the River, the lakes become smaller and, because you can see most of every part of them at a glance, seem to be intimate and friendly. In such places we occasionally see moose, huge beasts, upwards of six feet at the shoulder, who stand and stare at us curiously as we pass, perhaps the first humans they have ever seen. Mostly they are in the shallows near the shore, digging up water-lily roots, and often having their heads completely submerged, presently come up for air with a mighty splurge, and seeing us, stand a moment to watch, the water pouring in small cataracts from the pans of their wide antlers.

Invariably deciding that we are not to be trusted, they spin on their heels with surprising agility for so large an animal and lurch away at a springy, pacing trot that is a deal faster than it looks; and the noise of their going, once they hit the bush, is something like that of a locomotive running loose in the underbush.

At noon we arrive at the Ranger's Headquarters on Bark Lake. This is a large body of water, beautiful with its islands, inlets and broken, heavily timbered shores. At various points a number of streams enter the lake, and to follow the shore-line and discover all of them would take a week or more. Numerous routes, navigable by the methods we are using, lead off in all directions, and this lake is the gateway to an immense, little-known territory. From its outlet there flows the Mississauga River, small as yet—but don't worry; you'll find it big enough later on. So we got here, you see; we have made seventy-five miles in a day and a half. Not bad, admits Dougal, but if we'd have been getting up in decent time these last two mornings, we'd have been a lot farther. It's been fun, hasn't it. And now the serious work is about to start. After dinner we run, in quick succession, a number of small rapids. There is not much to them. This is only the beginning; the River is as yet young.

We pass several small lake expansions, and that night we camp beside swiftly running water, on the banks of the River proper. And all night, whenever we awaken, we can hear, in the distance, a dull, steady, ceaseless roar. Our first real white water, with all its unknown possibilities, lies just ahead of us. The next morning we arrive at the head of this. Part of the load is disembarked at the portage, as we will run with half-loads, taking only stuff that can stand a wetting. For this is a tough spot, and we will ship water, inevitably. We go to the centre of the stream again, set the canoes at the proper angle for the take-off. The canoes seem to leap suddenly ahead, and one after another, with a wild, howling hurrah, we are into the thick of it. Huge combers, any one of which would swamp a canoe, stand reared and birling terrifically beside us, close enough to touch. The backlash from one of these smashes against the bows and we are slashed in the face by what seems to be a ton of water; we are soaked to the skin, blinded by spray—on one side is a solid wall of water, there is a thunderous roar which envelopes us like a tunnel, a last flying leap and we are in the still pool below, safe, wet, and thrilled to the bone. It was a short, wicked pitch, and we have taken much water, in which we are now kneeling, but we have saved two loads on the portage, so it paid us well to run; and for you, I think the experience was worth the wetting. We go ashore, unload and empty out, carry the remaining stuff over the portage, load up and are away again—happy, with a great, new-found sense of self-reliance, and looking for more thrills. There are plenty.

The current has much increased in volume and

power. Rapid succeeds rapid in quick succession. Most of them we run, some full loaded, others with half loads, saving a lot of work on portages. A few are more in the nature of low waterfalls, or else too filled with stones, and are impossible. There is a marvellously picturesque cataract, running through a chasm in a series of chutes and sudden drops, that is worth the trouble of going off the portage to see. This spot is known as Hell's Gate. The old rapid is too dangerous to run with any load, and the canoes go down empty. No useful purpose is served in attempting these places, it being done only for the excitement to be got out of it. In such spots, brother, we leave you on the shore, and I think that the skill and daredeviltry, the utter disregard for personal danger with which a good canoeman flings (there is no other word) a good canoe from place to place through a piece of water in which it seems impossible that anything could live, will furnish you with a spectacle that you will be a long time forgetting. And you may sometimes, too, remember the narrow plot that is a grave, surrounded by a picket fence, at one of them. A man was drowned here a few years ago, an old, experienced trapper, who made perhaps this only one mistake in all his life. Some rivers have their private graveyards, to which they add from time to time. But Mississauga is not considered dangerous; there are portages round all bad places. We are only running them for the fun of it. We get wet quite often, and occasionally we have to step ankle-deep in water to make a landing. But things like that begin not to matter to you; it's all part of the game. You are by now becoming so used to these small hardships that to be too comfortable gives you an uneasy feeling of guilt. You say you have a sinking feeling at the pit of the stomach at the head of every piece of bad water; but I notice that you shout as loudly as the rest of them in the middle of it. Between rapids the River runs sometimes smooth and deep, at other places widens out into noisy shallow reaches, with scarcely depth enough to allow the passage of a loaded canoe; in such stretches the men get out and lead the canoes like horses. Frequently, a rapid stops abruptly to quieten down in a pool, deep and still and flecked with foam, where the River seems to pause awhile to reflect and lay new plans for the next wild and turbulent course.

We see no more moose but plenty of deer, and more than once we see a number of them together, standing ahead of us in the shallows, craning their necks, and weaving back and forth with very human curiosity, to get a better view. Sometimes they wait until the canoes are almost upon them before bounding through the shallow water with prodigious leaps and a great clattering and splashing, as they make for the safety of the tall timbers. One, a half-grown fawn, was encountered crouching in a pool, evidently in distress, and a wolf was seen hovering in the underbush on shore. A stop was made and the wolf routed, while

'*Bounding through the shallow water with prodigious leaps and a great clattering and splashing, as they make for the safety of the tall timbers.*'

the exhausted fawn was tied by all its feet, and trans-
ported to a safer neighbourhood and turned loose
again. Wolves, having chased a deer down to a river,
not infrequently separate, and one of them having
crossed over at another point, is there to meet the
deer when the latter swims across. Twice we see wolves;
one of them is swimming, and a frantic but unsuccessful
attempt is made to catch him before he lands, but he
has too much lead on us. We come suddenly on another
whilst he is drinking, and before he goes have time to
note that he does not lap the water, as does his kinsman
the dog, but drinks like a horse, by suction. He makes
stupendous bounds, far exceeding those of a deer in
length, for a deer leaps up and down, and a wolf leaps
ahead—which is one reason why a wolf can catch deer;
persistence and a rather high order of intelligence, as
well as an aptitude for learning by experience, being
the other contributing factors.

Well, we had our first argument, you and me, and
I supposed we both learned something. Oh, that's
nothing unusual. Sometimes everybody gets interested
and the whole brigade stops and argues like nobody's
business, about something that not one of them knows
anything whatever about. Just to be different. Anyhow, we made two or three miles in the meantime—
and say, there's a couple of bears, no, three of them,
an old lady and two cubs; get out your camera. They
won't do us any harm, naturally. (You'd best get that
bug-a-boo of 'wild' animals out of your head; they're

just being themselves, same as us.) The little fellows are all alive with curiosity to find out what we are, but their mother isn't even interested. Clowns of the woods, these black, woolly boys, with a thoughtless, rollicking, good-natured disposition, though it must be admitted that they are often thoughtless enough to go rollicking through someone's provision cache; but their heart's in the right place—it's just a way they have. No, I wouldn't get out of the canoe and pet the cubs if I were you; the old woman is probably not a mind reader, and she'd likely think you were going to hurt her youngsters and slap you down. Good way to start a bear story, but it will do you no good. Bears are quite a common sight here, swimming, or walking along on sandy beaches.

There are incidents. At a stop, where we are to make tea, Shorty, always unfortunate, sticks the tea-pail pole into a hornets' nest. The mosquitoes may not be what they were, but the hornets prove to be as good as ever, and we move away from that place. One of the canoes has its canvas badly cut on a sharp stone. The leak is a bad one, and the crew hustle their craft ashore, where the puncture is mended, temporarily, with soap. Gus, the financier, explains that this is the real reason why we carry soap; but don't listen to him —remember how he caught you on the jam question? But the outstanding presentation is the one provided by Zepherin when, carrying a canoe up a steep bank, he begins to slide backwards, canoe and all, towards the river again. He struggles futilely to regain traction, and being an active man he puts on quite a show, and goes through the most extraordinary gyrations to regain his footing. All hands are gathered at the landing, and the exhibition is watched with the greatest interest. Zepherin is a heavy man, the place is steep and slimy, he has a good start, and we all know that he hasn't the chance of a snowball in Egypt. He has a canoe with him, so if he falls into the river it will be quite all right with us. Zepherin, red in the face, feeling as ridiculous as a car-load of circus clowns, and still sliding, gasps out in desperation 'Simmering Cimmerian centipedes! None of you guys goin' to help me? see a fella' slide into this jee-hovally creek!' and goes on sliding, until near the edge he throws the canoe from him with a terrific imprecation and shouts 'I'll not go in! I won't go in!' and still he keeps on sliding, waving his fist at the scenery and bellowing 'You can't put me in! You can't pu——' and slides, with an uncommonly good display of footwork, over the brink and into about three feet of water. Spluttering like a walrus, he scrambles to his feet immediately, and standing submerged to the waist he shakes his two fists above his head and roars in a terrible voice, 'Put me in, did yuh?—but you can't keep me there, by cripes! —and I'll get out when I'm dam' good and ready, so I will! Try and stop me!!' and with a blood-curdling whoop he surges ashore. By this time we all began to feel the least bit uneasy as to how he is going to take

this, like small boys who have only too successfully
defied the authority of a policeman. But Zeph has
never actually killed a man—yet, and it is with some
relief that we see him sit down upon a stone, as he
enquires in his fog-horn voice, 'Why didn't some of you
mugs push me in so I could get it over with?' And
then he laughs and laughs until he can laugh no more.
So we laugh too, if you know what I mean—keeps him
from feeling self-conscious, don't you see? Dougal,
who enjoys, among the more superstitious, the doubtful
reputation of having once been seen at both ends of a
portage at the one time, now puts in an appearance, just
when he isn't wanted, and has observed the latter part
of our little true-life drama. Ever a man who could ill
brook delay or accident, he shoulders his way up to
Zeph and asks him what in the name of all that is
blind, black, and holy, was he fooling around in the
water for. Zepherin looks at him for a moment in
stunned silence, his cavernous mouth agape. 'What was
I fooling in the water for?' he repeats in a voice weak
with astonishment, and then louder, 'What for, you
say?' and then in a roar, 'Foolin' in the water, me!
Why, you pollusive, reptilian rapscallion—g'wan, you
runt yuh, or I'll make a pile of dog meat out of yuh,
that two short men couldn't shake hands over, so
I will'; and addressing the surroundings, one hand
raised in a supplicating gesture toward high heaven,
he asks, 'Did yuh hear that one, did yuh?' and calls
on all the powers to bear witness that he is an innocent

man. Whereat Dougal, unable to remain serious any longer in the face of such an absurd situation, bursts into laughter with the rest of us. Such is our discipline, the kind that will, with the right men, move mountains.

*　*　*　*　*　*

And so, day succeeding day, we go forward. And as we penetrate deeper and ever deeper into this enchanted land, the River marches with us. More and more to us a living thing, it sometimes seems as if it were watching us, like some huge half-sleeping serpent that observes us dreamily, lying there secure in his consciousness of power while we, like Lilliputians, play perilously upon his back. Until, to our sudden consternation, he awakens, as though some austere, immovable landmark that you had passed a thousand times before, should rise one day and look you in the face and ask you what you did there; so does this serpent, that is the River, turn on us unexpectedly, and writhe and hiss and tear, and lash out at us in fierce resentment at our audacity.

Here and there along its course are mighty waterfalls, some with rainbows at the foot of them; and one of these thunders down a deep chasm, down two hundred feet into a dark swirling eddy, seemingly bottomless, that heaves and boils below the beetling overhang as though some unimaginably monstrous creature moved beneath its surface. And in the vortex of this boiling cauldron there stands a pinnacle of rock on which no creature ever stood, crowned with a

single tree, for ever wet with the rainbow-tinted spray
that in a mist hangs over it, while the echoing, red
walls of the gorge and the crest of the looming pines
that overtop them, and the all-surrounding amphi-
theatre of the hills, throw back and forth in thunderous
repetition the awe-inspiring reverberations of the
mighty cataract. And as we stand and watch it, it is
borne home to us what a really little figure a man cuts
in this great Wilderness. Even Landreville has no
story to fit the occasion.

Long stretches there are of smooth, slow-flowing
water where everything is quiet. Here the shores are
level and in wide spots there are low alluvial islands
covered with tall, yellow, waving grasses, with blue
irises standing in amongst them, showing brilliantly
against the darker, gloomy back-drop of the heavy
timber. The River winds and twists much in such
places. The bends are not far apart and the curve of
the banks shuts off the view before and behind at no
great distance, so that we are constantly walled around
by trees and move inside a circle that never really
opens up but goes with us, as if we were passing
through a series of high-walled, tree-lined pools in
some old, forgotten moat, that looked every one the
same, save only for the ever-changing character of the
timber that enclosed them. We pass the cavernous,
high-vaulted forests of the hardwoods, full of long,
shadowy vistas that seem in their pale, green dimness
to be peopled with uncouth and formless shapes, and

that stretch vaguely off in all directions in an un-ending labyrinth of counterfeit roads that lead on to nowhere; then, the sepulchral gloom of spruce woods, muted corridors, that beyond a short distance from the River had resounded to no sound of human voice; and more pleasant, the poplar ridges with golden pools of sunlight on their floor, and interspersed with huge in-dividual pine trees, austere, towering and magnificent.

On the shores of the shallow, grassy lake we find the remnants of an ancient Indian town. A ônce proud flagpole had fallen in the midst of it and lay rotted beside the mouldering timbers, and good-sized trees grow within the moss-grown rectangle of what once had been Old Green Lake Post. On a low hillside, facing West, there is a graveyard and on one grave there stands a willow wand, and tied to it there is a tiny offering wrapped in yellow buckskin. It looks to have been quite recently placed there and arouses speculation; but we lay no finger on it and leave it quietly swaying there above its dead. And this evidence of remembrance and simple faith subdues even the rougher element among us. We wander round a little, and wonder who it was that lived here in those distant days, what trails they laid, and how the hunting was, how many of them there were who called this place their home. And the answers all lie buried in the graveyard, below the grasses on the sunny hillside, their secrets, and the swinging, beaded token, guarded by a regiment of pines.

Not far from here we meet a lone-fire Indian. He comes ashore as we are eating and drifts on soundless, moccasined feet to our fireplace and stands there for a moment, very still. 'I am Sah-Sabik', he says. 'The white men call me Yellow Rock.' He is ancient, and says that he had known the Post when it was young. Kebsh-kong he calls it, Place-Walled-in-by-Rushes; which it was. We had never seen him before but he knows us all each by name and reputation, by means of that old and very efficient line of communication, the moccasin telegraph. We suspect that the offering on the grave is his, but do not ask. He has no English, but some among us know his language; but he tells us little. He talks not so much to us but to himself, and speaks not of the present but of the past, the very distant past, and of the men beside whose graves we had so lately stood. So we give him some tobacco for a present, and in return he offers some strips of dried moose meat in a clean, white linen bag, which we accept. He allows us to give him some tea too, and some flour, provided, he says, that it is very little. He doesn't want to get a taste for it, because he has no means of getting any more. He lives the old way, asserting that the modern Indians eat too many soft foods (does this sound familiar?), have strayed from the way of their fathers, have become unmanly and have no guts. Hearing him, we wonder do all nations, tribes and generations of men so lament the ineptitude of the generation that follows them. His own

meagre resources suffice him, for your true Indian uses
sustenance merely as an engine uses fuel. For Northern
wild life, waters and the Wilderness are his existence
and aside from his few human relationships, the phe-
nomena and inhabitants of the wild lands are his
only interests, his perpetual occupation in which his
physical appetites are almost entirely satisfied. His
kind is rarely met to-day. A shadow amongst the
shadows in this Shadowland the Indian recedes, as
silently and as mysteriously, and as incalculably as he
came, and will soon be gone. And so we leave the old
man to his musing and his lonely recollections.

To-night, the travelling being easy down a steady,
uninterrupted current, we journey far and take our
supper late, and travel on by moonlight. And now
the forest that borders all the River becomes an eerie
place of indeterminate outlines and looming, un-
familiar objects that come and go, and rear themselves
up before us only to disappear on close approach. In
the darker spots the canoes become invisible and can
be only placed by the soft swish of the paddles; but
where the moonlight filters through the trees there are
pale shafts of illumination through which they pass
like ghost-craft, or things impalpable, seen only for a
moment, to disappear again. The spruce trees look
like witches with tall, pointed bonnets and sable cloaks,
and the white birches that flicker here and there among
them as we pass, shine whitely out like slim, attenuated
skeletons and in the shifting, garish moonbeams seem

gruesomely to dance. In these shrouded catacombs the fire-flies glow on and off with pallid phosphorescence, little lambent eyes that wink and blink at us like lights on dead men's graves; while ever beside us loom the crowded legions of the trees, and there is that feeling that we pass before an endless concourse of motionless onlookers, unmoving and unmoved, shadowy spectators who watch with a profound and changeless apathy from the tall pavilions of the pine trees. And the brigade seems to move in a world of phantasma and unreality, as though the River were some strange, unearthly highway in another world where tall, dark beings, shrouded and without faces, gaze featurelessly from the river-banks upon us and stare and stare, or loom over us with ghostly whispering while some, to all appearance, beckon with impish, claw-like hands to stay us, with a hideous suggestion of blind-men reaching for us in the dark; while behind them lies a vast Kingdom of Gloom of which they are the dark inhabitants, and in whose shadowy thoroughfares untoward events lie crowded, imminently, ready to happen.

And we pitch camp in a moonlit glade and make a bonfire, which drives away the wraiths and goblins and brings us back to commonplace reality, and we discover then that we are tired. So we go to bed and sleep till noon next day. The afternoon is spent overhauling canoes, putting an edge on paddles, so they will cut sharply and without splashing or resistance in a heavy current. Dry spruce poles are cut ten feet

long, are trimmed and smoothed and driven into short
sockets known as poling irons that give weight to the
pole and will grip a rock, and are used both in
descending and in climbing rapids, in water where
a paddle is of no avail.

These preparations are suggestive and a little
ominous, though you would not think so to hear the
crowd roaring with laughter as Red Landreville tells
the one about the calf that was born with a wooden
leg. But I don't hear you laughing, brother; you say
you feel that something is about to happen? Well, you
are right, something is—the smooth, uneventful stretch
is over. To-morrow we hit Seven League Rapids, the
Twenty Mile. What's that? You say it needn't have
come on quite so sudden, but that's what you came for,
isn't it? And you can't go back, so you've got to go
ahead. And besides, this is the high-light of the whole
trip, and you'll enjoy it—and if you don't, you'd better
not admit it.

Before second smoke the following morning, its deep
voice is carried back to us by the South wind. The
time of day is right, and the sun is in a good position
for running; everyone is expectant, and iron-shod poles
and extra paddles are placed firmly in position where
they will not be jarred overboard, but can be snatched
up at a moment's notice. For it will be fast work at
times, in some spots a matter of split seconds.

The distant mutter of the rapids as we draw near,
swiftly becomes a growl, grows louder, and increases

in volume by the minute, moving swiftly towards us,
rising up the scale of sound until it becomes a thunderous uproar. A hundred yards ahead the River
suddenly drops abruptly out of sight, breaking off in
a black, horizontal line from which white manes and
spouts of foaming water leap up from time to time;
below that—nothing, apparently, and the tree-lined
banks fall away at what, from that distance, looks to
be a most alarming angle. But now we feel the tug and
pull of the tow. No more talk.

The current, smooth as oil, deep and swift, carries
us in its irresistible suction towards the dark V of deep
water that marks the channel, and the canoes, driven
a little faster than the current to gain steerage-way, are
worked almost broadside on into this and at railroad
speed, one after another, are flung like chips into this
raging inferno of water. Are we going down sideways
on this dangerous curve in these light flimsy craft at
twenty miles an hour! Crossways, into this seething
vortex!! Yes, yes, we must, to fight the current, to
escape it and catch an eddy, for just ahead is a standing
rock against which the full force of the River hurls
itself in ungovernable fury, striking with terrific impact;
and towards this the canoes are dragged by the deadly
pull of the undertow, inevitably, inexorably. Crossways
in the current, canoes headed towards the opposite
bank, the crews dig deep with heavy, powerful strokes,
faces set, eyes intent on some object they are using for
a marker, using all the skill they know and straining

every muscle to tear loose from the grip of the current that is dragging them, inescapably it seems, towards destruction. Inch by inch we are gaining the necessary leeway—comes a sudden, sharp crack, faintly heard above the racket—a broken paddle! A canoe, out of control, whirls toward the rock—swiftly the man (he is alone) grabs another paddle. His life depends on how quickly he moves—now his bow is farthest out, still sideways, and going fast—Look at that! he throws himself forward into it, thus gaining a canoe's length, lifting the stern out of the current as his weight drives deep the bow—the canoe swings completely around and out, hurtling by the death-trap with only inches to spare. And then with a wild halloo the other canoes swing into line, head on, right to the edge of the current, and with whoops and yells of exultation the paddlers drive home into the thundering white water. A drumming sound passes swiftly, now it is far behind us—the rock— we have no time—confusion—an outrageous, dizzying medley of sound and furious action—snarling waves with teeth of stones, sheets of flying water, back-lash and hissing spume, the hoarse shouts of the white men and the high-pitched ululations of the Indians piercing the rolling drum-fire of the rapids. Men twist and heave and jab, and thrust with good maple paddles, throwing the canoes bodily, almost, from one strategic point to another, prying prow or stern aside from sure destruction. For this is Men against the River and all must run successfully. To fail means death. The bows-

'*Down its mad course go the Rivermen, carefree and debonair.*'

men throw themselves forward, sideways, backward, the sternsmen sometimes standing, sometimes crouching in the bottom, reaching forward or behind, the paddles of both cutting the water like knives, their blades beneath the surface for half a dozen strokes. Each man senses his team-mate's every move, and each responds with lightning speed and the lithe quickness of a cat, as the canoes career and plunge and pitch and the scenery goes reeling by, the trees an endless palisade on either side resounding, echoing and re-echoing with the roaring of the waters, a mighty close-packed concourse of immovable spectators, onlookers to the wild pageant of the River that races on between them in triumphant progress, decked with banners of white water and flashing crests of spray, and leaping waves like warriors, barbaric, plumed and shouting—this is the Twenty Mile.

And down its mad course go the Rivermen, care-free and debonair, wild, reckless, and fancy-free, gay caballeros riding the hurricane deck, rocketing down the tossing foaming River; a gallant, rollicking colour-ful array, my trail companions; Men of the Mississauga.

From *Tales of an Empty Cabin*.

## CHAPTER TWO

## The Winter Trail

OUT from town; the warmth, the laughter, the comfort left behind. Past half-finished barns, and snowy deserts of burnt stumps; past the squalid habitations of the alien, while the inmates stare out with animal curiosity; and so beyond the works of man, to where the woods become thicker and thicker, and all is clean, and silent, and shining white—the winter Trail.

Trees filing by in endless, orderly review, opening up before, passing on either hand, and closing in behind. That night a camp under the stars. Then, the hasty breakfast in the dark, breaking of camp in the knife-edged cold of dawn; shivering, whining huskies squirming impatiently whilst numb fingers fumble with toboggan strings, and the leather thongs of dog harness. Then away!

Strings of dogs swinging into line; a couple of swift, slashing dog fights, the shouts of the drivers, cracking of whips, and an eventual settling down to business. The swing and soft sough of snowshoes in the loose snow, the rattle of frame on frame. Then the sun rises. Glittering jewels of frost shivering on the pointed spruce-tops, like the gay ornaments on Christmas trees. The breath jets into the crackling air like little clouds of smoke, and steam rises off the dogs. Onward, onward, speed, speed, for the hands are still numb, and the cold strikes the face like volleys of broken glass; and we have far to go to-day.

So, for an hour; we begin to warm up. Suddenly ahead, the thud of a rifle, the answering crack leaping with appalling reverberations amongst the surrounding hills. Shouts up front; someone has shot a caribou. Good! fresh meat for supper.

Two of the more lightly laden teams drop out, and their owners commence expertly to skin and dress the kill; as their hands become numb they will plunge them to the elbows in the warm blood for a minute, and resume their work.

More hours; steep hills where men take poles and push on the load ahead of them, to help the dogs; on the down grades, tail ropes are loosed, and men bear back with all their weight, some falling, others dragged on their snowshoes as on a surf-board, amidst the shouts and yells of the brigade and the excited yapping of the dogs as they race madly to keep ahead of the flying toboggan. Meanwhile the Trail unwinds from some inexhaustible reel up front, passes swiftly underfoot and on behind, while the trees whirl swiftly by.

Then another stop; what is this? 'Dinner', say the trail breakers; well, they ought to know, they are bearing the brunt of the work. Quick, crackling fires, tea made from melted snow, whilst the dogs take the opportunity to bite the ice balls off their feet; most of them are wearing moccasins, evidence of thoughtful owners; for men, red or white, have always a heart for a dog. Pipes are lighted, and all hands relax utterly and smoke contentedly—for a few minutes.

Meanwhile, a word for the husky. Lean, rangy, slant-eyed and tough as whalebone, hitched in teams of four; over muskegs and across frozen lakes; tails up, tongues hanging, straining against the harness, bracing themselves at the curves, trailwise and always hungry, these faithful animals haul their loads all day for incredible distances. Not overly ornamental in appearance, inclined to savagery and deadly fighting, and thieves of no mean ability, these half-bred wolves are as necessary to transport in the North as horses were in the West in the early days. On more than a few occasions, they have been the means of saving life by their uncanny knowledge of ice, and unerring sense of direction.

And now the short rest is over, and we swing into position as the teams go by, and are away. Hours, miles, white monotony, and a keen, steady wind; lake and portage, gully and river bank; sometimes the crest of a bare hill from which a fleeting glimpse of the surrounding country is obtained. Limitless, endless, empty distance before, behind, and on either hand.

Later a trail turns in from the left, a thin winding ribbon, dwindling to a thread, to nothingness, across a lake, the far shores of which show but faintly, coming from out of the Keewaydin, the storied, mystic

North. The trail is well packed by snowshoes of all sizes, men, women and children; Indians.

Good going now; the trail breakers, glad of the respite, drop behind. On the hard trail the snowshoes commence to sing.

Smoke ahead; teepees, windbreaks; the Indian camp. Sharp vicious barking, howling, and then an unspeakable uproar as a herd of wolf-dogs swoops down on the caravan. Shrill scolding of squaws, who belabour lustily with burning sticks, restoring comparative quiet. Black-eyed, round-faced children stand aloof, whispering in soft voices. Maidens with heads in shawls peep from canvas doorways; buxom old ladies declaim loudly, as they cook at open fires. A tall spare man with Egyptian features, and long black hair, intones gravely in an ancient language, and we understand that we are invited to share the camp ground; the place is well sheltered, and, we are told, there is much wood, and moose meat. But we cannot stay; the mail is with us, and travels on schedule; to-night we camp at Kettle Rapids, to-morrow at Thieving Bear.

'Will we take tea.' We surely will, for who can refuse tea on the Trail? Large steaming bowls, and strong.

Away again; more hours, more miles. The teams with the meat have caught up, and the party redoubles its speed; it is getting colder and the men commence to trot. The snowshoes sing shriller now as the *babiche* tightens in the frost, and speed, and more

'*Away again; more hours, more miles. Speed, and more speed is the slogan.*'

speed is the slogan. Another lake; long, narrow, and bordered by glittering spruce trees garbed in white; the great sun, hanging low above them, dyeing their tops blood-red.

And as the sun goes down, the shadows creep softly out of the woods to the feet of the runners, and beyond. The wind drops and the cold quickens. One man drops out; there is blood on his moccasins. Incorrectly dressed, his feet have chafed with the rub of the bridles and have been bleeding for an hour. Another man steps aside and joins the first; as no one of the brotherhood of trail runners can be left alone in distress; an unbreakable law. But the mail man is satisfied, so all hands stop for the night.

Out axes and after the drywood, boy! A mighty clamour of steel biting into wood. Large piles of spruce boughs make their appearance. Semicircular wind-breaks of canvas stretched over poles cluster before a central fire, eight feet long. Smoke billows up to a certain height, to open out in a spreading, rolling canopy over the camp. Dogs are fed with frozen fish or moose meat, this their only meal in twenty-four hours.

It has now been dark a long time, but wood is still being cut; eventually quiet settles down and men sleep; but not the dogs. It seems they never sleep. One of them finds a morsel of something eatable; a swift rush and he is fighting at least six others. Howls, snarls, sharp, shrill yapping as of wolves; then curses, shouts, thuds, and silent scurrying retreats; for your husky does not yelp when beaten, but is a skilful dodger.

Once more, quiet. And then the moon rises, pale, and very large, and seemingly no farther away than the back of the next ridge, the ragged outline of the shrouded trees standing sharply out across its face.

From around the fire, where each takes his turn at replenishing, come sounds of sleep. The bizarre shadows cast by the shifting flames dance in and out the tree trunks, and white snowshoe rabbits appear and disappear silently within the circle of light, unseen by the dogs who have crept up near the fire, dozing with the eye nearest it.

The moon rises high and resumes its normal size. The cold grips the land with the bite of chilled steel; trees crack in the frost like scattering rifle-fire. Then, later, as the moon sets, a thin wailing comes stealing across the empty wastes, wavering in strophe and antistrophe, increasing in volume as voice after voice takes up the burden; the song of the wolves.

A little later the mail man gets up, scans the stars, and pronounces it time to rise. An hour and a half, or less, and all is ready. As the day breaks, the last team disappears around a bend in the Trail. And nothing remains but a few bare poles, flattened piles of brush, and a dead fire, and, stretching either way into the chill, white silence, the Trail.

Such, in normal circumstances, is the Trail in winter. A few days' soft weather, however, or a rainstorm, may bring conditions which make travelling virtually impossible. Yet a man caught out in such shape must do the impossible; he must go on. Goaded on by the knowledge of a rapidly diminishing food supply, or the certainty of more bad weather, he must keep moving; for this is the Trail, and will be served.

One season, having located a pocket of marten and lynx, which, being within a short distance of the railroad, had been overlooked, another man and myself hunted there all winter. We made frequent trips to town, a distance of twelve miles, often covering the route in four hours or less.

Hearing from a passing Indian that there was talk of a close season being suddenly declared, we decided to take out our fur, and dispose of it while it was still legal, and so avoid a heavy loss. This was late in April, and the ice was on the point of going out, but there were yet four feet of snow in the bush.

We started before daylight one morning, so as to cross most of the lakes before the sun took the stiffening out of the night's frost. There was open water of varying widths and depths around the shores of every lake, and we crawled out over this on poles, drawing the poles with us for use in making our landing. A light blow easily punctured the ice in any place, excepting on our winter Trail, which, padded down solid by the numerous trips back and forth to town, formed a bridge over which we passed, most of the time erect, and with little danger. An hour after sunrise, a south wind sprang up, the sky clouded over, and it commenced to rain. The bottom went out of the ice bridges, necessitating walking the shores of each remaining lake, and on land the trail would no longer support our weight.

Where we had so blithely passed at a three-miles-an-hour gait in winter, we now crawled painfully along by inches, going through to the knee at each step, the snowshoes often having to be extricated by hand. The surface held until we put just so much weight on it, when it let us through at every step with a shock that was like to jar every rib loose from our backbones. Off the trail the snow was of the consistency of thick porridge, and progress there impossible.

We heartily cursed the originator of an untimely close season, who, no doubt, sat at home in warmth and comfort, whilst we, his victims, wet to the skin, our snowshoes heavy with slush, our feet and legs numb with ice-water, crept slowly on. The water slushed in and out of our porous moccasins; but there was little we could do beyond wringing them and our socks out, and so occasionally getting relief for a few minutes, and also keeping moving. At that, we were no worse off than the man who walked all day in ice-water with holes in his boots, claiming that he preferred them that way, as he did not have to take them off to empty them.

Every so often we made a lunch, and drank tea, and our progress was so slow that on one occasion, on making a halt, we could look back, and still see the smoke of our last fire, made two hours before. And this is to say nothing of the load. We took turns to draw the toboggan, which could not stay on the trail, since the sides having given out it was peaked in the centre. Thus the toboggan ran on its side most of the time, upsetting frequently, and the friction producing, contrary to common supposition, cold instead of heat, it became coated with ice, and drew with all the spring and buoyancy of a water-soaked log. Frequent adjustments had to be made to snowshoe-bridles with numb hands, the increased weight of the snowshoes breaking the tough leather repeatedly.

Resting was not desirable, except at a fire, as we became chilled to the bone in a few minutes; and, dark coming on with several miles yet to go, we pressed on as best we might. The jar of constantly going through the trail was nauseating us, and we had almost decided to camp for the night in the rain, when there loomed up in the gloom a large grey animal, standing fair in the centre of the trail ahead. We reached simultaneously for the rifle, but the animal came towards us with every appearance of confidence, and turned out to be a big Indian dog, out on a night prowl for rabbits.

Had this occurred in days gone by, no doubt we should have subscribed for a shrine at the place, in honour of some saint or other; as it was we said nothing, but seized the unfortunate beast, and quickly stripping the tump-line off the toboggan, with multiple knots fashioned a dog harness, and hitched up our new-found friend. Showing no regret for his interrupted hunt, he hauled along right manfully, whilst we, unable to do enough for our deliverer, kept the toboggan on the Trail, as far as was humanly possible, with poles. About that time, the wind changed to the North, the sky cleared, and it commenced to freeze, and with all these things in our favour, we made the remainder of the trip with ease, having spent seventeen and a half hours of misery to cover about ten miles up to that point.

In the woods nothing can be obtained except by effort, often very severe and prolonged, at times almost beyond human endurance. Nothing will occur of its own volition to assist, no kindly passer-by will give you a lift, no timely occurrence will obviate the necessity of forging ahead, no lucky accident will remove an obstruction. Of course, a man can always give up, make fire, eat his provision, rest, and then slink back to camp, beaten and dishonoured; but that is unthinkable.

As you sit on your load to rest, searching the sky-line for some encouraging indication of progress, it is borne home to you most irrefutably that all the money in the world cannot hire a single hand to help you, and that no power on earth, save your own aching feet, will cause the scenery to go sailing by, or take one solitary inch off the weary miles ahead. And as you sit in chill discomfort, your body bowed down from the weight of your load, your mind depressed by the incubus of the slavish labour yet to do, you realise that the longer the rest, so much longer you remain on the Trail. The thought goads you on to further efforts. Those packs will never move themselves, and the fact that they may contain skins worth a small fortune obtains for you no respite.

In civilisation, if you showed your peltries, attention would be showered on you; willing hands would lift you to your feet. Deep in the forest your valuable pack becomes a useless burden, except for the pinch or two of tea and the few bites of greased bannock it may contain, which are worth, to you, more than all the gold in Araby.

At times you are fain to give up, and abandon your hardly won treasure, of which you would give the half for one mile of good footing, or the privilege of going to sleep for an hour. But you must struggle on; exhaustion may be such that further movement seems impossible, or you may have injuries that cause exquisite torture with every movement; but that trip must be finished, or, in the latter event, fire must be lighted and camp of some kind made.

From *Men of the Last Frontier*.

## CHAPTER THREE

# Risks of the Trail

THE hardships and privations of the trapper's life have developed in him a determination, a dogged perseverance, and a bulldog tenacity of purpose not often necessary in other walks of life. At the outset, before the commencement of the hunt, the trapper may have to spend one or two months in getting supplies to his ground, after spending most of the summer searching for a likely spot. His exploration work is of great value to those who follow him, but it is all lost time to him. He expects, and receives, nothing for his labours, but counts it all in the day's work, and hopes his ground will produce the goods. On such trips these men are sometimes called on to perform seemingly impossible feats, and probably no trip coming inside my recollection would illustrate this better than the journey undertaken by a white man and an Indian, three winters ago in Northern Quebec.

These men came from farther south and, having made no allowance for the difference in climate, on their arrival found the freeze-up already in progress. Travelling during this period is considered by even the most enduring as being almost, if not quite, impossible.

Nothing daunted, these two hardy souls commenced their pilgrimage, for it was nothing less. Each had a canoe-load of about 600 lb. On the first lake they found ice, which, whilst not capable of bearing a man, effectually prevented the passage of a canoe. This had to be broken, the two men armed with poles first breaking a channel in an empty canoe, from one expanse of open water to another. This entailed the unloading of 600 lb. of baggage on any kind of shore, into the snow, and the reloading of it on the return of the empty canoe; work enough, if frequently performed. They proceeded thus at the rate of about three miles a day, carrying the loads and canoes over seven portages. It snowed steadily day and night, increasing the difficulties on portages, making camping out a misery, and preventing at the same time the ice from becoming thick enough to walk on.

For five days they continued this struggle, making camp every night after dark, soaking wet and exhausted. It now turned colder, and this did not improve the ice under its clogging mass of snow water, while in the channel so laboriously broken, the cakes of ice and slush often cemented together, during the return trip, into a stronger barrier than the original ice had been. Held up at length on the shores of an eight-mile lake by these conditions they passed around the entire shoreline of one side of the lake on snowshoes, the ice being too weak to carry them otherwise, and even then, within a few feet of the shore, driving their axes through the ice at one blow every few feet. A full day was consumed on the outward journey, and they returned by the light of a clouded moon, splashed to the head, their garments freezing as they walked. But they were well repaid, as the water flooded the ice around the holes they had cut, and slushed up the snow on it. The whole mass froze through, forming a kind of bridge, over which they passed in safety, drawing the canoes and loads in relays on improvised sleighs.

This style of progress, alternating with the usual portages, continued for several more days, one man going through the ice in deep water, and being with difficulty rescued. The men were in no danger from starvation, but wrestling with hundred-pound bags of provisions under such trying conditions, and carrying ice-laden canoes over portages on snowshoes, was too severe a labour to be long continued. Worn-out and discouraged by their seemingly hopeless task, too far in to turn back, not far enough advanced to remain, faced by the prospect of passing the best part of the winter on a main route denuded of game, these companions in tribulation plodded with bitter determination, slowly, painfully, but persistently ahead.

Mile by mile, yard by yard, foot by foot, it seemed, those mountainous loads proceeded on their way, as two steely-eyed, grim-faced men opposed their puny efforts to the vindictive Power that vainly inhibited their further progress.

Their objective was a fast-running river, some forty miles in from the railway, knowledge of which had caused them to retain their canoes, in the hopes of finding it unfrozen. This proved to be the case, and on its current they travelled in ease and comfort, as far, in two days, as they had previously done in the two weeks that they had been on the trail. When the water no longer suited their direction, they camped several days to rest up; and winter coming on in real earnest, they cached their now useless canoes, and making sleighs moved on into their ground by easy stages.

From *Men of the Last Frontier*.

\* \* \* \* \* \*

A timely sense of humour has taken the sting from many a bitter misfortune, for out on the endless Trail, the line between tragedy and comedy is very finely drawn. A look, a word, anything that will crack a laugh in faces drawn with anxiety, no matter at whose expense, will often make a burlesque out of what would otherwise be an intolerable situation.

For instance, no one could ask for a more humorous and elevating exhibition than I myself once gave, before an interested audience of sixteen Fire Rangers. Upset by an unfortunate move, for which my partner and I were equally to blame, I swung out of the canoe as it capsized, keeping hold of the stern, and going down the rest of the swift water like the tail of a comet, amidst the sarcastic comment of the assembled Rangers. My bowsman was wearing heavy boots instead of moccasins, and in a kneeling position, the usual one in a canoe, his stiff footwear had become wedged beneath the thwart. He must have been almost a minute under the overturned canoe, unable to extricate himself, and in grave danger of drowning, when, with what little assistance I could give, he somehow got loose. Bewildered, he climbed on to the canoe, which, being old and heavy, immediately sank, and me with it.

I am an indifferent swimmer, if any, and this was a dangerous eddy, and deep; there were no hand holds to speak of. So, although it rolled and twisted considerably in the cross current, I stayed with the canoe, on the chance that it would float up, as without it I would be a dead loss anyhow; and soon my head broke water again. The attentive concourse on the river bank, who were in nowise disturbed, evidently thinking we were giving an aquatic performance for their benefit to lighten the cares of a heavy day, were highly diverted, until my companion, on my return to the surface, swam ashore, where his condition apprised them of the true state of affairs. In a matter of seconds a canoe was racing towards me, whilst its occupants shouted encouragement. About this time I was in pretty bad shape, having taken much water, and my hold on the canoe was weakening; so I commenced to shout lustily, suggesting speed. To my horror, one of the men suddenly ceased paddling and commenced to laugh.

'Say', said he, 'why don't you stand up?'

And amidst the cheers and shouts of the appreciative assemblage, I stood up in about three feet of water. I had been floating with my legs out ahead of me, and had drifted backwards within a few yards of the shore.

Then there is the official whom I saw sitting in a canoe which had run aground and filled. Wet to the waist, he sat in the water with both feet elevated above the gunwales.

'What are you doin' there?' angrily demanded his assistant, who stood on the rock, submerged to the knees.

'Keeping my feet dry', replied the official with chattering teeth.

Many of the prospectors are old 'desert rats' and plainsmen, used to horses and knowing but little about canoes. One such, not realising the chances he was taking, attempted the negotiation of a difficult piece of fast water with the loaded canoe, whilst his companion crossed the portage. Unable to distinguish the channel, the prospector ran foul of a swift shallows; and, on getting out to lighten the load, he was swept off his feet and nearly carried away. The canoe swung sideways and filled to the gunwales, and, with part of its contents, was salvaged only after an hour's hard work. An inventory was taken of the remaining goods, which were found to be thoroughly soaked. The man who had walked did not berate his crestfallen companion, who was responsible for the mishap, merely remarking disgustedly:

'We needn't have gone to all that trouble, we could have got that stuff just as wet letting it down on a rope.'                From *Men of the Last Frontier*.

\*  \*  \*  \*  \*  \*

*" What are you doin' there?"* angrily demanded his assistant.
*" Keeping my feet dry",* replied the official.

It is a serious misfortune, nay, a catastrophe of sweeping proportions, for a trapper to be burnt out, or see his territory going up in smoke. I know whereof I speak, having had the distress of seeing the greater portion of a well-loved and familiar landscape destroyed by a fire in the space of forty-eight hours, I myself and several others barely escaping with our lives; and this necessitated my moving out of the district entirely. I was in the Fire Service at the time, and on going out to the village for provisions was detained by the Chief, as smoke had been observed in a district with which he knew me to be familiar. That same evening an Indian, having paddled fifty miles without stopping, save for portages, came in and reported the exact location of the fire, which had come from somewhere south and west, and was fast eating its way into my hunting ground.

The next day a gang of hastily hired rangers and Indians started for the scene of the trouble. The main route was very circuitous, and more than once my fortunate knowledge of the presence of beavers enabled us to make use of several short-cuts, the dams being in good condition, and the shallow creeks, otherwise unnavigable, being well flooded. With these things in our favour we arrived within ten miles of our objective late on the first day and we began to hear the roar of the fire. That night, as we camped, sparks and large flakes of dead ashes fell into the tenting ground, and the sky was lit up by the terrible, but beautiful and

vivid glare of a sea of flames. Much delayed by
numerous portages, it was not until noon the next day
that we were within measurable distance of the conflagration. There was a considerable mountain between
us and the fire, and along the foot of this we tugged
and hauled heavily loaded canoes up a shallow river,
plugged with old fallen timber. Sparks, brands and
burning birch bark fell about us unheeded. Sweating
white men cursed and heaved, and passed scathing
remarks on the owner of the country who did not keep
his rivers in shape—myself. Patient, silent Indians
juggled canoes and their loads with marvellous dex-
terity from one point of least resistance to another. Men
of four nations waded in mud to the knees, broke
paddles and ripped canvas from canoe-bottoms, un-
reprimanded by an eloquent and forceful Chief.

At his desire I described a short route to the fire area,
and he swiftly made his plans and disposed his forces.
My allotted sector, with two Crees, was the mountain,
at the foot of which a couple of men made camp. Once
up the mountain, from which we had a plain view of
the camp, we separated, each taking a different direction, in order to get three observation angles on the fire
from the eminence. Once alone, and in a fever of
anxiety concerning my possible losses, I plunged ahead
at full speed, angling towards the greatest volume
of sound. I must mention here, that being used to
moccasins, I was much hampered by a pair of stiff
hard-soled larrigans which I had donned for fire-

fighting purposes, and in which at times I was at some pains to keep on my feet.

I was suddenly startled by the sight of a bear which lumbered by me, bound for the river. A rabbit raced almost between my legs, then another and another. The roar had become deafening, and the heat almost unbearable, and I strained every muscle to attain the western, or far, crest of the mountain, before it became untenable for my purpose. I saw another galloping rabbit, and noticed curiously that it was passing from the left, when it should have been coming head on. A partridge flew, again from my left, struck a tree, and fell to the ground, scorched, blinded, and gasping. It I killed in mercy.

Just then I detected a sharper undertone of sound underlying the deeper heavy roar ahead of me, and on looking to the left and behind me, towards the line of flight of the bird, from whence it seemed to come, I saw the thin crackling line of a ground-fire creeping swiftly towards me like a molten carpet, now within a hundred yards of me, and backed at no great distance by a seething wall of flames. The fire had met me more than half-way, and had thrown out a flanking party. I was neatly trapped.

I turned and incontinently fled, making for the widest part of the V of flames, as the main conflagration had now caught up. And here is where my hard-soled packs came in. Unused to boots, I found I could not run on the slippery jack-pine needles without losing

time, and it took all of whatever will-power I may
possess to tone my movements down to a swift walk,
and curb my desire to race, and scramble, and tear my
way regardless of boots, direction or anything else, just
run—run. The flames were now on three sides of me,
and my clothes were becoming brittle. Fortunately the
intense heat kept the smoke up so that if I could keep
my distance I was in no danger of suffocation; the
danger lay in a very probable enveloping movement by
the enemy.

I saw some harrowing sights. Dumb creatures en-
deavouring to save their lives from the one element
against which all are helpless, some succeeding, others
not. I saw tiny partridges in huddled groups, some
lying on their backs with leaves in their claws, beneath
which they deemed themselves invisible, realising that
there was danger somewhere, and using the only protection that they knew. And—I know of no greater
love that a mother can have than this—I saw the hen
bird sitting dumbly by, unable to herd the little
creatures to safety, waiting to burn with them.

The smoke darkened the brightness of noonday, but
the cavern of flames lit up the immediate surroundings
with a dull red glow. I was keeping ahead of the fire
but my direction began to be a matter of doubt.
'Follow the animals', I kept thinking; but all that
could had gone by, and now there were no more. I
forced back my terrible fear. I caught myself saying,
'You can't make me run, you—you can't make me

run', and there I was running and slipping and stumbling in my deadly footwear; and with a jerk I slowed, or rather accelerated, to my swiftest walk.

More partridges, eyeing me dumbly from low limbs, and the chicks huddled beneath: oh the pity of it! Two more rabbits: follow them, follow them, fast! A small muskeg showed up; I raced for it, expecting a pond: there was none. Past the muskeg and on. The growth of small cypress that cluttered the forest here became very thick. Surrounded by smoke, now commencing to billow down with the back-draught of the fire, my brain reeling with the heat, with the horror of what was too probably to be my funeral pyre driving me on, I scrambled desperately ahead, with no thought but to keep the advancing flanks of the destroyer behind me.

My feet seemed leaden, and my head a shell, light and empty, as I squirmed with desperate contortions to force a way through the continuous barrier, like a cane-brake, of small trees. I could no longer keep any specific direction, but knew I must now be far past the camp. I thought momentarily of my two companions; I had long since passed the area they had been assigned to. And then, breaking at length through the last of the barrier of saplings, I burst out on to the eastern brow of the mountain. Fire goes but slowly down a hill, so I took time to breathe, and looking down could see the camp; and from its proximity I knew that my ordeal by fire had not lasted over twenty minutes, if that, though I would have sworn that it had occupied an hour.

The camp ground itself was a scene of the utmost confusion. Tents were being pulled down by main force and jammed into canoes, sometimes poles and all; pots, blankets, baggage and equipment of all kinds, seemed, at that distance, to be picked up in quantities and dumped on to the nearest craft.

I descended the mountain, the fire commencing to creep over its edge, and found waiting for me with a canoe one of the Crees who had gone up with me. He had seen me coming out on the summit, expecting me there as he watched the course of the fire. He grinned and spoke in English:

'Hot like hell, eh?'

'Some', I replied soberly, as I felt the split and scorched back of my canvas shirt.

On the river just above the camp was a live beaver-dam, and it came as a timely assistance in aiding us to make our getaway, deepening the river so that we reached without loss of time a mile and a half portage leading inland to a large lake. This, one of my main trails, was in good shape, and we moved over it at nothing less than a trot. To check the fire was impossible without a change of wind, and in any case reinforcements were necessary.

From *Men of the Last Frontier*.

\*    \*    \*    \*    \*    \*

Three years ago, on a night in spring, a man went down from his camp fifty yards to the river to get a pail of water and has never been seen since.

A year before the time of writing, in this district, a deer-hunter took an afternoon stroll and was discovered eleven days later by one of a gang of twenty-five men who scoured the woods for him for twenty miles around.

In the first case the man strayed off the water-trail in the dark, and not arriving at the shack he attempted to correct his mistake and took a short cut, only to arrive back to the river at another point. He again endeavoured to strike the camp but, angling too much to his right, missed it. So much was learned by the finding of the pail at the river bank, and by his tracks. After that he entered a country of burnt, bare rocks, and small patches of green swamp, and he is there yet.

The second man, having killed a deer, remained where he was, erected a shelter and kept a fire. Beyond the mental strain incident to his adventure he was in good condition, when found. Wherein lies the secret of the difference between being correctly and incorrectly lost.

The safest course, with night coming on, and being still astray, is for one to stop, make a fire, and as comfortable a camp as may be, and wait for daylight, with the feelings of security that it brings after the uncertainties and exaggerated forebodings of a long night. Then, perhaps, bearings can be taken to better advantage, and the sun may be shining, although it may now, after half a day of extended and aimless ramblings, be impossible for the wanderer to determine in which direction a start should be made.

From *Men of the Last Frontier.*

\*     \*     \*     \*     \*     \*

Hardship is a comparative term, according to habit and environment. I once was a guest in a house where something or other fused, and the electric lights went out. For those people it was a real hardship, perhaps the first time that some of them had known, and very well I could appreciate this, as it was certainly highly inconvenient, if not in some degree dangerous. It was as though a person had gone suddenly blind, than which, aside from the thought of impending torture, I can think of nothing more terrifying. For I have been blind, out on a frozen lake at night, alone.

It was a matter of eight miles to the nearest human being, but eight miles is as good as a hundred if you are blind, out in the snow-bound Wilderness. Early that morning I had left from the last settlements. I was lucky enough to get a lift from some freighters who were going in with supplies for a party of surveyors. It was not at all cold, a state of affairs that made bad snow-shoeing, but was very comfortable weather for enjoying a ride, something I didn't often have. That night the freighters made camp some miles from a cabin, where I intended to sleep, and I refused their invitation to stay with them, and slipping into my snowshoe-bridles started off. There were signs of a possible storm and some of the men urged me to stay; but travelling at night, even in a storm, held no terrors for me, I supposed, and away I went. For a little time after leaving the warm, ruddy camp fire, with the congenial company gathered around it, the portage trail felt very lonely and dark and cheerless, and I almost turned back once or twice. However, with the concentrated attention to business that night travelling demands, I had little time for vain regrets and the feeling of lonesomeness soon passed. I then noticed that it was getting colder; all the better snow-shoeing, thought I; which it was.

Arriving at the end of the portage, I discovered that the wind had changed to the North. Quite a stiff breeze was blowing, but there were no clouds. The waning moon, pale and on its back, the half averted face upon it pinched and sunken like the visage of one dead, gave out a pallid illumination that helped very little to distinguish the features of the landscape. The lake was about seven miles across, and on its far shore stood the cabin I was making for, and giving my snowshoe-bridles a few twists to tighten them, I started across the wide expanse of lake.

The snow was badly drifted into hard irregular waves, and the sickly light of the recumbent moon was worse than none at all, constantly deceiving my eyes, so that I stubbed my snowshoes on the brittle crests of snow waves or else stepped out on to nothing, to land with a back-breaking jar in a trough. This was very tiring and I had to go slow at last, becoming so fatigued that I even considered going ashore, making fire and passing the night there. But the shores on either side were a couple of miles or so away, and I was now well over half way up the lake towards my destination. Moreover the wind had now freshened and was getting stronger every minute, and I had no idea of what it might portend before morning came. It presently increased to a steady gale that was neither blustering nor boisterous, but that blew with a cease-less, changeless velocity that had the sweeping drive of a rushing wall of water and, in my tired condition, was nearly as irresistible. This wind was from the North and blew somehow dry and brassy, hard as sandpaper, and cut like a buzz-saw, even through my stout buck-skins. Between the freezing, tearing wind and the continual stumbling over the snow-billows I was rapidly becoming exhausted. My eyes began to burn, and it seemed as if the wind was drying them, so that when I shut them and walked some distance with them closed, as I was now obliged to do from time to time, they felt as though filled with hot sand.

Presently I noticed that when looking straight ahead the shore on my right was, for some reason, getting dim. Now, I knew it to be only half a mile away as, hoping for a certain amount of shelter, I had been veering towards it for some time; while the shore on my left, at least three miles away, was plainly visible out of the tail of the other eye. Before long I found that unless I turned and looked at it directly the right-hand shore showed only as a grey, shapeless wall. This struck me as strange, and not a little disturbing, and I hadn't gone very far when the other, more distant shore became dim, turned grey and disappeared entirely. I looked up, I couldn't see the moon. And then dawned upon me the realisation that I was going blind! I could still see my snowshoes, and they were covered with new snow; I looked down at my buckskin shirt, it was white with snow—yet no snow was falling on my face; perhaps it was frost. I tried to brush it off; it wouldn't come. I turned up the shirt and looked inside; it was white too—that was it! my eyes were turning slowly white, everything else was turning white —eyes that could see only white—white blindness, the terrible White Death I'd heard the Indians talk about!

I stood for a few moments and let this sink in. Then I made for the shore while I could still distinguish it. In my haste, unable to see the snow with my bleaching eyeballs, I tripped and staggered, and fell repeatedly. I wanted to get close enough so I could hear the gale roaring in the timber on the shore, otherwise if it too should disappear, I might not ever find it. I was surrounded by a wall of white save in this one direction. But I got there, just about in time, for as I approached it seemed to melt, dissolve away from either side, leaving in front of me only a narrow strip of grey, that stood upright before me. I remember thinking that it looked like a great grey bastion, and had the effect of being round as the sides fell away to where they were invisible; and this I watched as it too began to shrink, turned white and receded into nothingness. And I pawed the air to feel for it after it was gone, and I stumbled forward with outstretched hands to find it, this, my last link with the living world; and I ran a step or two and crashed into a tree and fell upon my back there, in the snow.

And I knew then that I was blind. I knew all the stark horror, the awful helplessness, and the unutterable anguish of one stricken suddenly blind. I scrambled to my feet as the ghastly, inescapable FACT roared like thunder through my reeling intellect, that it had got me, that I was blind—white-blind! My snowshoes were off and hung around my ankles and as I stood I sank to the hips in the snow, and cried out, a terrible, animal sound, the agonised cry of some creature in a trap, my fists clenched above my head, staring out with my sightless eyes, trying to make them see. I must have been in a little bay, for there was no wind there, and that awful, demoniacal yell came back to me and I yelled again in aswer to the echo, and while my face ran with perspiration I shouted 'I am blind, blind, do you get it? I am BLIND!' And the echoes answered 'I am blind—am blind—blind—blind.' And a demon came and whispered 'You are blind', and beat at my brain and the frenzy passed and my body became

*‘I shouted “I am blind, blind, do you get it? I am blind!”’*

pleasantly numb and warm, and I sat down com-
fortably in the snow and my eyes didn't hurt any more;
and I was very tired. And I thought this must be the
end; the end. It seemed strange to go out in this way
after having braved the Wilderness so long—so simple,
and after all, so easy. And I remember thinking that
if I was found, no one would ever know what it had
been all about.

And then all at once I came out of my lethargy, and
muttered to myself that I was not going to be found in
the Spring spread out on the beach like a dead toad,
but decently, with my weapons and my snowshoes
beside me, kind of natural looking. What puerile things
we think of in extremity! But I had lost my rifle and
axe, and crawled around in the snow and felt for them,
but could not find them. So I wallowed a little further
inshore, my snowshoes dragging by the bridles, and ran
into a large tree. With a snowshoe I dug a hole in the
snow, at the foot of it, crawled in there, stood the
snowshoes up beside it, then pulled as much of the snow
in on top of me as I could. Thus I would sleep; and
nothing else seemed to matter. The wind had now died
down, and without it I could never find my way and
would perhaps wander bewildered on the lake until I
dropped from exhaustion. Better this, the cleaner way.

Reader, do not judge me, not until you have had a
like experience. There was not the heat of battle, nor
the heroic intoxication of some deed of valour or self-
sacrifice. I had taken the field once too often against

the power of Nature, had pitted my puny strength against the Wilderness; and this time I had lost. Just one more animal who must submit to the invincible decrees of the creed he lived by—the survival of the fittest. A small error in judgment had proven me unfit; I should never have started out from the freighters' camp. However, I was to get another chance.

Some hours later I awoke with a start, and stood up. At every move sharp daggers of pain shot through my muscles. I knew what that meant—I was beginning to freeze. I cursed myself for waking up. Now it had to be all gone through again. Water was streaming from my eyes and they felt as though on fire. I had tied my black silk neckerchief over them and this I now took off, and opened them.

It was with a distinct shock that I found that I could see; but that was about all. I could with difficulty make out shapes of tall grey spectres that stood about me, looking like huge columns wrapped in wool, enormously thick; these no doubt were trees. In one direction there was a faint glow, as of a candle light seen through a piece of flannel; this, I supposed, was the moon. My snowshoes resembled twin tombstones and when I reached for them I missed them by a foot or so.

Well, if I was going to see, there was no use in dying. Everything was very dim and hazy and distorted, and every object appeared to be coated with wool, or of enormous size. But I could see—enough to make a fire, beside which I sat on a bed of balsam brush until my sight was sufficiently restored to move on. I worked on my eyes, opening and shutting the lids, massaging them, and mopping the stream of water that flowed from them. The balls felt rough, as if corrugated. Slowly, painfully, they resumed their office, even though imperfectly. All this took a long time to do, and I found myself weak and almost incapable. A little more and I would never have got away from there.

Owing to its fictitiously exaggerated size everything I reached for eluded me, and it would have looked strange to an onlooker to have seen me clawing away at things that were six or eight inches from my hands; under any other circumstances it would have been an interesting experience.

Towards morning I collected axe and rifle and after a rather severe ordeal arrived at the cabin.

The tips of all my fingers were frozen, and I didn't see very well for several days. But I had learned a very useful lesson, and had perhaps found out the reason why men of known skill and proficiency in Winter travelling have been found, unaccountably, dead.

From *Tales of an Empty Cabin*.

\*     \*     \*     \*     \*     \*

## CHAPTER FOUR

## *Bears*

WASKESIEU is a tent city situated on the shores of a lake of the same name, a lake the far end of which is invisible to you as you stand on the broad expanse of sandy beach, some hundreds of yards in length, that stretches before this town of tents. The farthest you can see is at a point where the shores taper down from the bold, spruce-clad hills on either side, and nearly meet, forming a narrows only a bow-shot across, and even this point, in the middle distance, is visible only as a long, low line that shimmers in the sunlight of a Summer day. And far off as you may consider this, when you get there you are still only half-way up the lake.

Standing on the beach at Waskesieu, you begin to have a faint idea of the real meaning of the word Distance. Thirty miles from the camps, and beyond the distant narrows, accessible only by water, is Ajawaan Lake, where my Beaver People and I have our home in one of Canada's greatest Wilderness playgrounds, Prince Albert National Park.

Far enough away to gain seclusion, yet within reach of those whose genuine interest prompts them to make the trip, Beaver Lodge extends a welcome to you if your heart is right; for the sight of a canoe approaching from the direction of the portage, or the appearance of some unexpected visitors on the mile-long trail that winds through the forest from larger and more navigable waters, all coming to bid the time of day to Jelly Roll and Rawhide and their band of workers, is to me an event of consuming interest. Save for my animal friends I live here quite alone, and human contacts, when I get them, mean a lot, and are important.

The whole region is one vast Wilderness of lake and forest, and you may pass beyond the boundaries of the Park (if twenty-three hundred square miles of country is not enough for you) and never know the difference, and you can go East and West for unthinkable distances, and North as far as the Arctic Circle, with little interruption save that provided by the trading posts.

Every Spring the tent dwellers move into Waskesieu, and every Fall move out again, leaving this vast, unpeopled territory to the Mounted Police, the Park wardens, the teeming wild life population and myself. And perhaps the most interesting of all these Summer visitors are the bears. Waskesieu has bears of all kinds—excepting grizzlies—from little fellows of a hundred pounds or so, just youngsters starting out in life, to others that will go six hundred pounds—by no means the largest—just good, comfortable-sized bears, if you get what I mean. There are black ones with red muzzles, black ones without red muzzles, reddish brown, dark brown, and just plain brown bears, and I have seen some that were a rich bronze colour. They are inoffensive, good-natured fellows, who pay not the slightest attention to anybody, and it is no uncommon thing to meet a bear or so walking peacefully along the highway. The streets of the tent city are lighted up at night, but the lights are some distance apart, and it has been suggested that more lights be provided so the bears can see their way around and not get scared stiff by having people bump into them in the dark. They forgather around the various cook-shacks in groups of half a dozen or more, nosing around among the scraps that the cooks throw out for them, acting towards each other with an unfailing courtesy which it is very elevating to observe, and politely ignoring the sight-seers, who are getting the thrill of their lives and who, at a distance of about twenty feet, get all the bear pictures they could ever wish for. Some of these bears, the bigger ones, are regular visitors every year, and must be nearly worn to the bone from being photographed.

There is a seventy-mile highway between Prince Albert and the tent city of Waskesieu, that runs bang through the bush for the last forty miles of its length, and there is a spot, near the resort, where a she-bear and her cubs (one of those ferocious she-bears we hear so much about) will wait for cars, and if you stop for them the entire family will come over and beg for titbits in the most barefaced fashion. This, of course, rather discredits a lot of good old-fashioned traditions concerning bears, but the occupants of the car get quite a kick out of it, and can truthfully say thereafter that they are able to look a bear in the face.

Some of the younger set, among the newer bears, before they become thoroughly acquainted with the regulations, indulge in some rather ill-considered pranks, such as entering unoccupied tents and falling asleep there or getting their heads in garbage cans and having to be extricated; and a lady of my acquaintance entered her camp to find in it what she thought was a large black dog, who was making himself very much at home, and who regarded her entrance with supreme indifference. Somewhat nettled by this cavalier behaviour, the lady administered a severe drubbing to the intruder first with the flat of her hand and then with the broom, only to discover of a sudden that it was no dog at all, but a middle-sized bear, who behaved with admirable restraint, and allowed himself, so to speak, to be swept out of the house.

Yet another had, during his wanderings, been unchivalrous enough to annex a pair of ladies' shorts. He played with them awhile, but there was no kick in them, and quickly tiring of the pastime he moved off to fresh adventures. However, his claws had become entangled in the material and he could not detach it, and every so often he would stop and try to shake it loose, sometimes standing erect to do so, waving the offending piece of apparel at arm's length above his head, like a flag. He went through the most extraordinary contortions to rid himself of his encumbrance, and his

'*Another had, during his wanderings, been unchivalrous enough to annex a pair of ladies' shorts.*'

evident embarrassment at his inability to remove it was highly diverting to onlookers. Eventually the garment flew high in the air and landed on the branch of a tree, and the bear, greatly relieved, looked at it fixedly for a moment and kept on going.

Then there is the one who is said to have attached himself to the hotel, and every day, at a certain hour, he would walk most unconcernedly into the kitchen. He being rather a large bear, the staff would walk just as unconcernedly out. Arrangements were always made for his accommodation, the odd pie and so forth being left out for him to eat, in order that he would not burglarise the premises. Having eaten he would walk out in a state of the greatest gratification, and the staff would then walk in, also with a good deal of satisfaction, and not without some feelings of relief. So everybody was quite cheerful about the whole business.

Sometimes a store-house gets broken into, but this is generally by the lower and less educated type of bear. No real harm is intended of course, it being really the fault of the night watchman who omitted to leave the door open. However, no bear who knows his onions, or has at least a grain of self-respect, will do this, it being more ethical, and also a deal less labour, to beg his meals at the cookery.

There is a report comes from one Summer resort (not Waskesieu!) that certain bears, wrongly accused of wilful damage and being victims of misunderstanding by the grown-ups, have been caught playing clandestinely with the children. How far these misunderstood bears would go in their endeavours to make themselves better appreciated is problematical, but probably no further than to take whole parties of youngsters on their backs for rides into the country.

Your bear is really a good fellow, and will eat almost anything that you give him, or that you may inadvertently leave lying around, just to show you that his heart is in the right place. He has a humorous outlook on life, and a few minor depredations should not be allowed to detract from his character. He expects you to be very broad-minded; and why not? That bears sometimes break open provision caches and take out bags of flour, scattering the flour all over about a half an acre of land and rolling in it, proves nothing except that bears are playful in disposition and like to roll in flour. I will admit that a bear who behaves in this manner should be severely reprimanded, but a judicious display of several quarters of beef, or choice hams, or a few jars of honey tastefully arranged so as to catch the eye (leave the jars closed, the bear will open them himself quite easily), will divert the bear's attention and prevent this sort of thing, for the time being at least.

Seriously, these bears give rather an atmosphere to the place, and are considered by most of those who see them, to be one of the chief attractions there. Some few timorous souls might not perhaps relish the idea of meeting a whole troop of bears on a main street, but for every one who doesn't, there are twenty that do. The bear is the clown of the woods, clumsy, and often a thief, but he is amiable enough if not abused; and it says a good deal in his favour that with bears in some numbers constantly present around the resort at Waskesieu, apart from certain ludicrous and quite harmless incidents, there has never been an accident.

## CHAPTER FIVE

# *Moose*

STILL-HUNTING (stalking) is an art learned from the Indian, an accomplishment in which few white men excel, save only those who have spent many days in the lodges of those silent, thoughtful people, or consorted much with those who have. I can almost hear the howl of protest going up from a host of pseudo-bush-men, whose experience is confined to running moose down in deep snow, blundering on them in sections where they are numerous, or shooting them at the water's edge, which anybody can do. I repeat that the average white man is not a good still-hunter.

There are exceptions; famous guides, celebrated for their skill in 'calling', crafty as the savage whose tricks they have acquired, men who have earned a reputation of never coming out without their moose, are to be met in bush communities in all parts of Canada; but they are as outstanding there as is a genius in a colony of artists. But all must take off their hats to the Indian. His own evasive, subtle mind fits him admirably to cope with the cunning and elusive nature of such animals as moose and deer. Indeed, it is probable that his type of mentality has been evolved by just such exercises during many generations, for the red man is primarily a hunter. Few but he are able, without snow, and in most cases even with it, to track and locate a moose without scaring the animal (in which case he is gone, and as impossible to overtake as a train would be), for no moose, unless bogged to the shoulders in snow, has ever been taken by tracking him down from behind. Not all are mentally fitted to enter into the intricacies of move and countermove, advance, circle, and retreat which must be studied in each case, or to guess the necessary allowance for the changing of a scarcely perceptible breath of wind.

Busy workers have not the time to acquire the knowledge that warns of too close an approach to a disadvantageous firing position, nor have they, unless they live as close to Nature as their swarthy brethren, the instinct that shows itself in the achievement of knowing the exact position of the moose in relation to himself, before the last two or three steps are to be made that will expose the hunter, and give him his shot at a quarry that he has stalked for an hour. And all this without sight, sound, or indication of the presence of moose, excepting perhaps some week-old tracks and nibbled branches, and in a section, such as moose commonly resort to, where a man is lucky to be able to see ten feet ahead of him.

It takes no little skill also to enter a 'yard' of moose, padded down with tracks as numerous as those of cows in a pasture, and make a specific set at one particular beast. Yet this is necessary; hit or miss, rambling tactics meeting with no more success than firing into the

centre of a flock of ducks ever does. The least careless-
ness of approach, the rattle of cartridges in the pocket,
the slapping of a twig on the clothing, or even too much
mental concentration on the animal itself, causing uneasiness, will alike result in a sudden flurry and crackling
of twigs and brush, the measured, rapidly diminishing
thump of hoofs driven by legs working like piston-rods,
the distant crash as some rotten tree gives way before
the driving weight of flesh, bone, and muscle, and then
utter silence. And like as not without a hair of the
quarry having been seen.

The actual shooting is child's play. More moose are
killed at fifty feet by good hunters than at a hundred
yards by good shots. A moose is not a hard target, and
once seen, looms up amongst the undergrowth like the
side of a barn. The difficult part is to get to see him.
On the still-hunt the sum and substance of the hunter's
efforts are to see the animal before it sees him; to
closely approach a moose without his being aware of
your presence is an impossible feat, as indeed it is with
any other of these dwellers amongst the leaves. But
like all the other types of deer, unless rendered frantic
by the scent of man, his curiosity gets the better of him;
he will stay until he gets a fleeting glimpse of what he
is running away from. That is the hunter's only chance
of success.

All animals that live in the wilderness are provided
with a set of protective habits which the skilled hunter,
having knowledge of them, turns to his advantage.

Beavers, when ashore, post a guard; not much advantage there, you think. But standing upright as he does in some prominent position, he draws attention, where the working party in the woods would have escaped notice. Both beaver and otter plunge into the water if alarmed or caught in a trap (in this case a stone is provided which keeps them there, to drown). Foxes rely on their great speed and run in full view, offering excellent rifle practice. Deer contrive to keep a tree or some brush between their line of flight and their enemy, and the experienced hunter will immediately run to the clump of foliage and shoot unseen from behind it.

Moose feed down wind, watch closely behind them but neglect to a certain extent the ground ahead. When about to rest they form a loop in their trail, and lie hidden beside it, where they can keep an eye on it, manœuvring to get the wind from their late feeding ground. These things we know, and act accordingly. We decide on the animal we want, and make a series of fifty-yard loops, knowing better than to follow directly in the tracks, the end of each arc striking his trail, which is a most tortuous affair winding in and out as he selects his feed. We do this with due regard for the wind, all along his line of travel, touching it every so often, until we overshoot where we suppose the trail ought to be. This shows—provided our calculations are correct, our direction good, and if we are lucky—that our moose is somewhere within that curve. It has now become a ticklish proposition.

We must not strike his tracks near where he is lying down (he cannot be said to sleep), for this is the very trap he has laid for us. If we go too far on our loop we may get on the windward side (I think that is the term; I am no sailor). Pie for the moose again. Probably he is even now watching us. To know when we are approaching that position between our game and the tell-tale current of air is where that hazard comes in which makes moose-hunting one of the most fascinating sports.

All around you the forest is grey, brown and motionless. For hours past there has been visible no sign of life, nor apparently will there ever be. A dead, empty, silent world of wiry underbrush, dry leaves, and endless rows of trees. You stumble and on the instant the dun-coloured woods spring suddenly to life with a crash, as the slightly darker shadow you had mistaken for an upturned root takes on volition; and a monstrous black shape, with palmated horns stretched a man's length apart, hurtles through tangled thickets and over or through waist-high fallen timber, according to its resisting power. Almost pre-historic in appearance, weighing perhaps half a ton, with hanging black bell, massive forequarters, bristling mane, and flashing white flanks, this high-stepping pacer ascends the steep side of a knoll, and on the summit he stops, slowly swings the ponderous head, and deliberately, arrogantly looks you over. Swiftly he turns and is away, this time for good, stepping, not fast but with a tireless regularity,

*'A monstrous black shape, with palmated horns stretched a man's length apart, hurtles through tangled thickets.'*

unchanging speed, and disregard for obstacles, that will carry him miles in the two hours that he will run.

And you suddenly realise that you have an undischarged rifle in your hands, and that your moose is now well on his way to Abitibi. And mixed with your disappointment, if you are a sportsman, is the alleviating thought that the noble creature still has his life and freedom, and that there are other days and other moose.

I know of no greater thrill than that, after two or three hours of careful stalking with all the chances against me, of sighting my game, alert, poised for that one move that means disappearance; and with this comes the sudden realisation that in an infinitesimal period of time will come success or failure. The distance, and the probable position of a vital spot in relation to the parts that are visible, must be judged instantly, and simultaneously. The heavy breathing incidental to the exertion of moving noiselessly through a jungle of tangled undergrowth and among fallen timber must be controlled. And regardless of poor footing, whether balanced precariously on a tottering log or with bent back and twisted neck peering between upturned roots, that rifle must come swiftly forward and up. I pull—no, squeeze—the trigger, as certain earnest, uniformed souls informed me in the past, all in one sweeping motion; the wilderness awakes to the crash of the rifle, and the moose disappears. The report comes as a cataclysmic uproar after the abysmal silence, and aghast at the sacrilege, the startled blue-jays and whiskey-jacks screech, and chatter, and whistle. I go forward with leaps and bounds, pumping in another cartridge, as moose rarely succumb to the first shot. But I find I do not need the extra bullet. There is nothing there to shoot. An animal larger than a horse has disappeared without a trace, save some twisted leaves and a few tracks which look very healthy. There is no blood, but I follow for a mile, maybe, in the hopes of a paunch wound, until the trail becomes too involved to follow.

I have failed. Disaster, no less. And I feel pretty flat, and inefficient, and empty-bellied.

Worst of all, I must go back to camp, and explain the miss to a critical and unsympathetic listener, who is just as hungry as I am, and in no shape to listen to reason. Experiences of that kind exercise a very chastening effect on the self-esteem; also it takes very few of them to satisfy any man's gambling instinct.

* * * * * *

A big bull racing through close timber with a set of antlers fifty or sixty inches across is a sight worth travelling far to see. He will swing his head from side to side in avoidance of limbs, duck and sway as gracefully as a trained charger with a master-hand at the bridle, seeming to know by instinct spaces between trees where he may pass with his armament.

It is by observing a series of spots of this description that a man may estimate the size of the bull he is after.

The tracks of bull and cow are distinguishable by the difference in shape of the hoofs; the bull being stub-toed forward, and the cow being narrow-footed fore and aft. Also the bull swings his front feet out and back into line when running; this is plain to be seen with snow on the ground of any depth; furthermore the cow feeds on small trees by passing around them, the bull by straddling them and breaking them down. Tracking on bare ground is the acme of the finesse of the still-hunt, especially in a dry country; and tracking in winter is not always as simple as would appear. More than a little skill is sometimes required to determine whether the animal that made the tracks was going or coming. This is carried to the point, where, with two feet of snow over month-old tracks, visible in the first place only as dimples, an expert may, by digging out the snow with his hands, ascertain which way the moose was going; yet to the uninitiated tracks an hour old present an unsolvable problem as to direction, as, if the snow be deep, the tracks fill in immediately and show only as a series of long narrow slots having each two ends identical in appearance. The secret is this, that the rear edge of the hind leg leaves a sharper, narrower impression in the back end of the slot than does the more rounded forward side. This can be felt out only with the bare hands; a ten-minute occupation of heroic achievement, on a windy day on a bleak hillside, in a temperature of twenty-five below zero. Nevertheless a very useful accomplishment, as in the months of deep snow a herd may be yarded up a mile from tracks made earlier in the season.

But should the herd have travelled back and forth in the same tracks, as they invariably do, we have confusion again. In that case they must be followed either way to a considerable hill; here, if going down-hill they separate, taking generous strides, or if uphill short ones. Loose snow is thrown forward and out from the slots, and is an unfailing guide if visible, but an hour's sharp wind will eradicate that indication save to the trained eye.

Assuredly the hunt is no occupation for a pessimist, as he would most undoubtedly find a cloud to every silver lining.

There are many ways of killing moose, but most of them can be effected only at times of the year when it would be impossible to keep the meat, unless the party was large enough to use up the meat in a couple of days, or, as in the case of Indians, it could be properly smoked.

In the Summer when they come down to water in the early morning and late evening, moose are easily ap-proached with due care. They stand submerged to the belly, and dig up with the long protruding upper lip the roots of water-lilies, which much resemble elon-gated pineapples. Whilst eyes and ears are thus out of commission the canoeman will paddle swiftly in against the wind, until with a mighty splurge the huge head is raised, the water spraying from the wide antlers,

running off the 'pans' in miniature cataracts, when all
movement in the canoes ceases, and they drift noiselessly like idle leaves, controlled by the paddles operated
under water. The moose lowers his head again, and the
canoes creep up closer now, more cautiously, care
being taken not to allow the animal a broadside view.
On one of the occasions when he raises his head the
moose is bound to become aware of the danger, but
by then the hunters have arrived within rifle shot
of the shore; so, allowed to provide his own transportation to dry land, he is killed before he enters the
bush.

In the mating season moose may be called down
from the hills by one skilled in the art, and threshing
in the underbrush with an old discarded moose-horn
will sometimes arouse the pugnacity of a reluctant bull;
but when he comes it is as well to be prepared to shoot
fast and straight.

After the first frosts bull moose are pugnaciously
inclined towards all the world, and more than one man
has been known to spend a night up a tree, whilst a
moose ramped and raved at the foot of it till daylight.
Whether these men were in any actual danger, or were
scared stiff and afraid to take any chances, it is impossible to say, but I have always found that a hostile
moose, if approached boldly down wind, so that he gets
the man-scent, will move off, threateningly, but none
the less finally. Although the person of a man may
cause them to doubt their prowess, they will cheerfully

attack horses and waggons, domestic bulls, and even railroad locomotives.

Bull moose are quite frequently found killed by trains at that time of the year, and they have been known to contest the right of way with an automobile, which had at last to be driven around them. A laden man seems to arouse their ire, as a government ranger, carrying a canoe across a portage, once discovered.

It was his first trip over, and, no doubt attracted by the scratching sound caused by the canoe rubbing on brush as it was carried, this lord of the forest planted himself square in the middle of the portage, and refused to give the ranger the trail. The bush was too ragged to permit of a detour, so the harassed man, none too sure of what might occur, put down his canoe. The moose presently turned and walked up the trail slowly, and the man then picked up his canoe again, and followed. Gaining confidence, he touched his lordship on the rump with the prow of the canoe, to hasten progress; and then the fun commenced. The infuriated animal turned on him, this time with intent. He threw his canoe to the side, and ran at top speed down the portage, with the moose close behind. (It could be mentioned here, that those animals are at a distinct disadvantage on level going; had the ranger entered the bush, he would have been overtaken in twenty steps.)

At a steep cut-off he clutched a small tree, swung himself off the trail, and rolled down the declivity; the

'He threw his canoe to the side, and run at top speed down
the portage, with the moose close behind.'

moose, luckily, kept on going. After a while the ranger went back, inspected his canoe, which was intact, and put it out of sight, and it was as well that he did. He then returned to his belongings to find his friend standing guard over a torn and trampled pile of dunnage which he could in no way approach. He commenced to throw rocks at this white elephant, who, entering into the spirit of the game, rushed him up the trail again, he swinging off in the same place as before. This time he stayed there. The moose patrolled the portage all the hours of darkness, and the ranger spent the night without food or shelter.

A moose, should he definitely make up his mind to attack, could make short work of a man. They often kill one another, using their antlers for the purpose, but on lesser adversaries they use their front feet, rearing up and striking terrific blows. I once saw an old bull, supposedly feeble and an easy prey, driven out into shallow water by two wolves, where they attempted to hamstring him. He enticed them out into deeper water, and turning, literally tore one of them to pieces. Fear of wounding the moose prevented me from shooting the other, which escaped.

When enraged a bull moose is an awe-inspiring sight, with his flaring superstructure, rolling eyes, ears laid back, and top lip lifted in a kind of a snarl. Every hair on his back bristles up like a mane, and at such times he emits his challenging call—O-waugh! O-waugh!; a deep cavernous sound, with a wild, blood-stirring hint

'*He enticed them out into deeper water, and turning, literally tore one of them to pieces.*'

of savagery and power. This sound, like the howling of wolves, or the celebrated war-whoop when heard at a safe distance, or from a position of security, or perhaps in the latter case, at an exhibition, is not so very alarming. But, if alone and far from human habitation in some trackless waste, perhaps in the dark, with the certainty that you yourself are the object of the hue and cry, the effect on the nervous system is quite different, and is apt to cause a sudden rush of blood to the head, leaving the feet cold.

Once, and once only, was I ever in any serious danger from the attack of a moose. On this occasion, needing meat, I was looking for moose-tracks. Finding some indications, I had, after only a short still-hunt, come on to two of them, a cow and a well-grown calf, at the edge of a beaver-pond. I shot the calf, which suited my requirements, it being yet warm weather, and the cow made two or three runs at me, but was easily scared away by a few shots fired in the air; I felt safe enough as I had in my pocket some spare cartridges, tied in a little buckskin bag to keep them from rattling.

Whilst skinning the kill I noticed a beaver swimming towards me, his curiosity aroused by the shooting probably, as I suppose that the crack of a rifle had never been heard before in all that region. The beaver was unprime, and the hide valueless, but, becoming interested in his movements, I sat down on the bank and watched him. Quite absorbed in my pastime I was suddenly startled by a slight crackling behind me, followed immediately by the hollow, coughing grunt of an angry bull moose. The sound was no novelty to me, but never before had it carried, to my ear, the note of menace that it now did. No thunderous bellowing roar of a lion could convey half the murderous intent expressed in the cold malevolence of that sound behind my back. It chilled me to the marrow, and the hair crept on my scalp. I jumped to my feet and whirled with a yell calculated to jar the horns off the creature's head, but which produced not the slightest effect. He stood facing me, every hair on his body erect, his eyes red with hate. He commenced rubbing his hocks together, sure signal of a charge, and I smelt distinctly the sickening, musky odour these animals emit when about to fight.

Afraid to make a sudden movement, for fear of precipitating an attack, I reached stealthily for my rifle, jerked it to my hip, pumping as I did so, and fired; that is, I pulled the trigger, and almost before the answering click told me the gun was empty it flashed into my brain like an arrow that I had emptied the magazine in driving away the cow.

But the spell was broken. The moose moved; so did I.

He had me between himself and the pond, with a margin of about ten feet in my favour. Once in the water, my chances I knew, would be poor; so I made pretty good time down the edge of it, and the moose ran parallel to me; we seemed to be pretty evenly matched for speed. At the end of the pond I turned, quickly jumped the creek, and made for a stretch of flat, steeply sloping rock, where I could not be cornered up; this was covered with a scattered growth of small jack-pines, which, whilst not large enough to climb, offered dodging facilities. This move brought the moose directly behind me.

Still running, I got out my bag of cartridges, and pulled the string with my mouth: the knot jammed; I slackened my speed and tore at the bag with my teeth, ripping it, and spilling most of the cartridges. Ramming a shell into the breech I spun quickly round to find that the moose had stopped also, startled at my sudden move, and at about the same distance as before. I took quick aim, ready to shoot, but his rage was spent, and his former pugnacity gave way to uneasiness. I knew now that the danger was over, although I was obliged to sting him in the flank before I could get rid of him.

\*    \*    \*    \*    \*    \*

Being accustomed to hunting on the plains, where the game is in pockets, in gulleys, river bottoms, or in bluffs of poplar or willows, and thus standing partly located at the outset, and where it is more a matter of good shooting than good hunting, I found the still-hunt, as practised by the Northern Indians, an entirely different proposition. I know of no set of conditions to which the ancient simile of the needle in the haystack could be better applied.

My first experience was a good many years ago, with

a young Ojibway, yet in his teens. He had all the quiet
and confident bearing that goes with conscious ability,
moved like a shadow, and addressed me not at all.
From the outset he was in no hurry, spending much
time listening to the wind above, and inspecting the
ground below, both apparently inconsequent proceed-
ings as there seemed to be no wind and the only visible
tracks, to the reading of which I was no stranger, were
old ones and plain to be seen. However, his tardiness
suited me as, coming from a territory where walking is
not popular, and with the slippery, stiff-soled moccasins
of the plains Indian on my feet, I was quite well
occupied keeping him in sight as it was, and sincerely
hoped nothing would occur to increase his speed.

We proceeded in a fairly direct line of travel for
maybe an hour, when on a sudden he stopped and,
motioning me to come, showed me the fresh track of a
cow moose. Our progress now became more circuitous
and rambling, and he wandered apparently quite aim-
lessly around, listening meanwhile for a non-existent
wind.

It was during the Fall of the year, and I found the
wonderfully coloured woods a fairyland after the bare,
brown prairie, and the dry harsh mountains protruding
from blistering belts of sand. I was having a good time
and, moose or no moose, the gyrations of my gnome-
like and elusive companion intrigued me to the limit.
Presently he stopped in a glade, and looked around,
smiling with the air of one exhibiting a long-sought

treasure. I also looked around, but did not smile, as I recognised the spot as the one at which he had discovered the moose track. I had been twisted often enough in my calculations in the wild lands to guess what that meant.

'Ki-onitchi-kataig, we are lost,' I said.

He shook his head, and pointing to the moose track held up two fingers.

So that was it, he had in the circling discovered another moose. I had not seen him go through any motions indicative of a person discovering anything, moose or man, but supposed he must know what he was about. Maybe, I reflected, if we went around again, we could add another moose to the tally, and then surround them and make a general slaughter. The stripling now made some preparations. He took off his outside shirt and his hat, tying a folded handkerchief of indefinite colour around his bobbed hair. He hung his discarded clothing, with his blanket-cloth gun-case on a limb, and this mark of confidence in his ability to find the place again induced me also to remove and hang up my coat and hat; it seemed we must be about to hurry.

But my elfin guide stood motionless, apparently lost in thought, formulating his plans; and as he so stood, a study in black and tan, and faded buckskin, under the bronze dome of a giant birch tree, I thought that if only some great artist were there with skilful brush to commit to canvas the wondrous colour scheme, the shades, the shadows, the slanting streams of subdued light, the attitude of my primitive companion, wild, negligent, yet alert, furtive almost, like the creatures he was hunting, the masterpiece would result that could well be representative of a race, and of an epoch that will soon be with the things which are no longer, lost for ever.

The moment passed and he moved on.

Our progress was now very slow. Twice I ascertained that we were covering short sections of our previous itinerary, back-tracking in spots, making endless half-circles on a base line itself anything but straight.

On our left came a breath of sound, a slight rustle, and on the instant the boy sank into the woods like a hot knife through butter. Presently he returned, smiled his thin smile, and made the sign of a fox's tail. More half-circles. He commenced testing for the wind with a wet finger, and crumbling dry leaves in his hands allowed the dust to drift. The result was almost imperceptible. He seemed to gather some satisfactory information from the manœuvre, however, as he nodded his head and went on.

Bars of sunlight hovered here and there as the trellised roof of leaves wavered and swayed, and in the more open spaces it filtered through, to lie in golden pools upon the forest floor. These he skirted stealthily, keeping in the gloom on their borders with that instinct of self-effacement which, alike to the predatory or the furtive, spells success or safety.

He tested for wind more frequently now, on one occasion stopping and creeping backwards on his tracks, as though backing out of some sacred precinct that he had inadvertently entered. He circled out, and back into the same spot by another direction, a matter of yards only, and, selecting a spot in a wall of small evergreens, suddenly raised his rifle and fired.

At the same instant I saw a patch of coarse hair resolve itself into a huge brown body, as a cow moose surged through the balsams, blood streaming from nose and mouth, to sink down within twenty feet.

The Ojibway blew the smoke out of his rifle.

'Meheu', he said, speaking for the first time. 'It is done.'

From *Men of the Last Frontier*.

\*     \*     \*     \*     \*     \*

Animals as a whole are apparently devoid of imagination, which is fortunate for them as it enables them to meet the hardships they have to undergo with greater equanimity than can a man, and without any effort of will; but I have none the less been long convinced that, in many species, they are capable, to a more or less limited degree, of the power of thought. Even those of us having the most dim and distorted views on animal mentalities must concede something to the ape, the elephant and the beaver, and in many cases to the dog and the horse, but a long experience has hitherto failed to reveal to me any evidence of reasoning powers in any branch or individual of the deer family coming under my notice. The moose would seem to be a creature of slow mental processes, but that he is capable of using and does, on occasion, use his head, over and above his accustomed, almost automatic reactions, has been amply demonstrated to me and to others who have seen him, by an eight-year-old bull who has been a constant, if irregular visitor here for nearly five years.

At the time of writing he is lying alongside my canoe placidly chewing the cud with occasional grunts of satisfaction. The canoe, behind which he is ensconced, offers him a certain amount of shelter from the easterly wind that is blowing, though he could get better protection from it in the rear of the cabin, where he occasionally bedded down last year. But this new position perhaps has more intriguing possibilities, as he can see all that is going on, including my own small affairs, in which he seems to take a lively interest. In his present situation he is an object of curiosity and some resentment to the numbers of squirrels and whiskey-jacks that frequent this spot, and he is apparently quite undisturbed by the erratic movements of these small but rather violently active creatures.

Although I knew of the presence of this bull in the district on first taking up my abode here, and often had fleeting glimpses of him, I made no attempt at any friendly overtures and adopted a policy of quiet withdrawal on sighting him.

That Summer it became necessary to fell a number of

poplar trees to provide light for photographic work, and he made furtive nocturnal visits to the fallen trees for the purpose of eating the leaves. These visits to the free lunch counter thus provided continued as long as the leaves lasted, a matter of nearly two weeks, and during that period I made it a practice to be unobtrusively present at his feeding time. From then on, at intervals, he could be seen passing at no great distance from the cabin, and on occasion stood gazing down at it from some point of vantage. Often I observed him hovering on the hill-tops no great distance away, as I came and went on my constant patrol of the beaver-works. He even ventured beyond the last fringe of the forest that borders the tiny clearance on every hand, and watched me cutting wood, silent and motionless as the trees themselves. I did not press the matter, nor did I abate my labours, but carried on as though unaware of his presence, as evidently his interest was already sufficiently aroused. It was noticeable that the movements of the beavers seemed particularly to engage his attention, and one evening he came boldly down and stood observing them. The beavers speedily collected in a body and treated him to a salvo of tail splashing and stirred the water to a great commotion. All this had no effect on the moose whatsoever, except to cause him to step a little closer to see what it was all about.

Now a bull moose weighs something short of half a ton and is altogether rather a staggering proposition to have around at such close quarters and could, if he chose, become the least bit unmanageable; so becoming a little dubious as to the outcome of this rather alarming intimacy I stepped out of the cabin, having so far watched the performance through a window. With no hesitation the moose spun around on his heel and fled up the hill, and I commenced calling to the beavers in my usual manner to calm them. And now occurred the most remarkable feature of this whole business. At the first sound of my voice the moose slacked down, slowed to a walk and stopped, and as I continued calling the beavers he slowly returned, coming most of the way back, and commenced feeding on a clump of alders that was handy to him. Unbelievably, the words and inflections I used to pacify the beavers seemed to exert the same influence on the moose. On being further alarmed by my rapid movements the moose withdrew once more, but he did not go so far as before and was reassured by the same sounds, so that he again commenced to feed where he stood and spent upwards of an hour browsing unconcernedly around before he finally moved off. This, to me, unprecedented behaviour on the part of a wild animal with whom I had hardly even a bowing acquaintance, seemed very marvellous at the time and unless we are to admit that he figured the situation out for himself, an adequate explanation is hard to come by. I can claim little credit in the conduct of this affair, as the moose seems to have formed his own

decisions and acted on them. I pondered long and
deeply on the subject, and not yet satisfied, experi-
mented time and again during the now frequent visits
of this strangely complaisant beast and on most occasions with the same result, scaring him by a sudden
appearance and easily recalling him. And each re-
hearsal was a further confirmation of what I scarcely
could believe myself was true, that without any attempt
at training or the exertion of any influence on my part
this astonishing and unfathomable creature, wild, free
and beholden to me for nothing, would respond
willingly to my voice, and place himself in my power
at a word. Fortunately this has occurred on different
occasions before a number of witnesses, otherwise I
would have some diffidence in committing the matter
to paper, and an unusual aspect of animal psychology
would go unrecorded.

During the past Summer and Fall the bull spent a
good deal of his time within the camp environs strolling
around complacently amongst my arrangements, the
woodpile, store-tent and canoes, etc. He sometimes
stood outside the cabin door for long periods, close
enough that some visitors were not unreasonably afraid
that he might try to enter. I was not too sure myself as
to what lengths this enterprising animal would go, as
he had already got, at the one time, all four of his feet
into a small canoe and smashed it beyond any possi-
bility of repair. I actually had to drive him away from
the door one night as his presence there, standing

engaged in some ponderous cogitations, was obstructing the passage of the beavers in and out of the cabin with their building materials. By this time they no longer feared him, but were probably like myself, a little uncertain as to what his next move might be, and refused to pass him.

Every animal has its special fear, both as a species and as an individual. In the case of this particular moose, his pet antipathy was to have anyone pass between himself and a lighted window, throwing thereby a quick flitting shadow across him. This would cause him to break away at a run, and although he could invariably be called back, he would retire hurriedly on the offence being repeated nor did he ever become accustomed to it.

Until the beavers began at last to accept this huge visitor as a regular feature, I always received fair warning of his approach at some distance by tail signals given out by the beavers. He has now become to them, I imagine, something of a necessary evil, to be tolerated even if not to be over-effusively welcomed, and he has become so ordinary that his presence is taken as a matter of course, and warnings are no longer given. And stepping out from the cabin into the night and almost falling, as I once did, over a beast the size of a horse, is a severe trial to the nervous system of any man, however bold.

While the weather was warmer, he had a habit of standing in the water at the landing, and whilst there, was evidently something of a spectacle to the young beavers, who would swim completely round him, slapping their tails on the water and creating a great uproar, all of which he would view with a lofty unconcern.

At times the behaviour of this strange beast led me to wonder if he was not lonesome, and that having at last found company that combined the advantages of being safe and at the same time interesting, he had attached himself to the place on that account. For animals of all kinds love entertainment, and become very excited and playful on the introduction of something unusual into the monotony of their everyday lives, and they seem to get much pleasure from the contemplation of something new and strange, always of course provided that it is first proven to be safe. This theory of a desire for social intercourse on the part of a dumb brute, I have long held to be as tenable as the better known and well attested one, that in some instances individuals of the brute creation will go to the opposite extreme, and become so unsociable as to be dangerous to their own kind.

This community of interest has no whit abated the native alertness and vigilance of this animal, as on my coming upon him once unannounced from behind a knoll he rushed immediately round to the far side of the little eminence and, using it for cover, beat a precipitate retreat. I cannot believe that animals under ordinary circumstances when running from danger do so in an excess of panic and blind terror. For scared as he certainly was, he must have retained an admirable presence of mind, as on my running to the top of the knoll and calling out loudly the pass-word, he stopped within a hundred yards and eventually permitted me to approach him; but being far from camp and in a section where he was not accustomed to encountering me, I did not put his confidence to too great a test. This is by no means the only evidence I have that animals, even when in full flight and apparently panic-stricken, have all their mental faculties working one hundred per cent, and I am positive that only when dominated by the mating instinct, or driven to extremes by hunger, or on finding themselves in some utterly unnatural situation, such as unwanted confinement, do they ever completely lose control of themselves.

At the earliest view I had of him, about five years ago, this now proud bull was little more than a spike-horn. He had only two V-shaped protuberances, each about a foot long, on his adolescent brow, which, as an abbreviated moustache sometimes does to an otherwise manly face, detracted from rather than added to his appearance of virility. The next year, however, he blossomed forth with a real set of antlers, his first, provided with a good-sized pan and several assorted spikes. In the mating season he strutted around with these in some style, and issuing loud vocal challenges that I am sure he was quite incapable of backing up.

Although he had been, at other times, a model of propriety and decorum, acting always the natural gentleman, with the coming of the first sharp frosts he was transformed overnight into something resembling a dangerous lunatic. He strode into view one afternoon with a demeanour greatly changed from his usual quiet and dignified bearing. He had about him all the appearance of one looking for trouble. With some idea of testing his courage, I brought out a birch-bark horn, an instrument shaped like a small megaphone and used for calling moose at this season, and gave a couple of short challenging coughs. The effect was instantaneous. With no preliminaries at all he opened hostilities on everything within reach. He tore at willows and alders, emitting hideous grunts, gouged and gored helpless prostrate trees, made wicked passes at inoffensive saplings that stood in the path of his progress, entered into a spirited conflict with an upturned stump, threw a canoe off its rack and had a delirious, whirlwind skirmish with a large pile of empty boxes. The clash and clatter of this last encounter worked him up to a high pitch of enthusiasm, and he gave a demonstration of foot-work and agility hardly to be expected from so large an animal. All this had a very depressing effect on the spectators, who consisted of several of my furred and feathered retainers besides myself—about the same effect that a crazed gunman running loose on a city street would have on the pedestrians. I tactfully withdrew with the horn, which

I carefully put away. Having, after a time, pretty well subdued all visible enemies, except the store-tent which he had fortunately overlooked, this bold knight moved off to fresh fields of glory, and from the way he surged through the scenery I judged it would not be very long before he got himself into serious trouble.

I viewed this exhibition with much the same feelings that would be mine were I to see a highly respected and respectable acquaintance suddenly commence to throw handsprings in a public place, or to roll a hoop along the street, shouting. There was also a certain feeling of pity for the temporarily aberrated mind that one feels in the presence of an inebriate, with more than a little of the same uncertainty.

For a week or more he failed to show up at the camp and I began to fear that he had met his Waterloo, but one evening on returning by canoe from a trip to my supply cache, I saw in the dusk the familiar dark, ungainly form reclining at ease before my cabin. My canoe was heavily loaded and the water was shallow, so I was entirely at his mercy, but he allowed me to land and unload without any argument, merely getting to his feet and feeding on the surrounding underbrush.

He does not come so often now and stays but a short time, an hour perhaps. By his actions, I think that he has succeeded in finding himself a partner. I cannot conceive by what system he was able to obtain her in a district so populated by big experienced bulls. He has no doubt all the optimism and enthusiasm of youth on his side, and perhaps he has met a cow who is, like himself, young enough to see romance and gallantry in the mock battles which this handsome young fellow no doubt staged before her, and to experience maidenly thrills to see him vanquish make-believe antagonists. And if he has made the same use of his brains in the selection of a mate that he did in his manner of adopting my domicile for refuge, he has no doubt picked himself a good one.

As he sits without, before the window, I see that he is gazing anxiously, wistfully back into the dark recesses of the woods. Ever and anon his head turns in this one direction, ears pointing, nostrils sniffing the air. And I know that back there his cow is lurking, afraid to come down into the open and brave the terrors of the unknown.

Soon he will follow the law of all nature and follow where his consort calls; and as he stalks majestically away, he will march as to the sound of drums and martial music, with regal pride and with the bearing of a king. For he has attained to his majority, has proved himself before the eyes of all the world. He is now a finished product from the vast repository of the Wild, a magnificent masterpiece of Nature's craft, scion of a race whose origin is lost in the mists of un-numbered ages, the most noble beast that treads these Northern forests.

From *Tales of an Empty Cabin.*

# GLOSSARY

*Abitibi.* This river flows from a lake of the same name, northwards into Hudson Bay from eastern Ontario.

*Ajawaan.* The lake where Grey Owl had his cabin. It is situated in the Prince Albert National Park, about one hundred miles north of the town of Prince Albert in central Saskatchewan.

*babiche. See* below, 'Snowshoe'.

*bannock.* A form of bread made with flour, water and baking-powder, baked in the ashes or in a fry-pan. Eaten fresh, and dipped in hot lard or pork-grease.

*bridle. See* below, 'Snowshoe'.

*brigade.* Consists of four canoes or more, but loosely applied to parties of any size.

*buckskin.* A soft leather made of deer or other skin. Caribou or reindeer skin does not stretch when wet. The buckskin jacket or hunting shirt keeps out the wind, remains soft, will not catch on thorns, and wears for ever. The fringes are not purely orna-mental, as in rain the water drips off them and the shirt dries better.

*caribou.* North-American reindeer.

*Cree.* A tribe of North-American Indians of Algonquin stock, like the Ojibways. The Crees occupied the region round Lake Winnipeg and the Saskatchewan River. Their chief enemies were the Blackfoot tribe.

*Fall.* Autumn; the season when the leaves fall. The term is chiefly used now in North America, but it is also an old English word.

*Fire Rangers.* These men are employed by the Canadian Govern-ment to patrol the vast forest areas to fight the menace of fire. Incalculable damage has been done, and is still done, by forest fires, which may devastate thousands of square miles of country. For a fuller description of the fire-service, the chapter entitled 'The Altar of Mammon' in *The Men of the Last Frontier* should be read. Aeroplanes are now used for patrol work, as well as an elaborate system of outlook towers, etc.

*Hudson's Bay Company*, generally known as 'The Company'. The history of Canada is bound up with that of the H.B.C. The Company was founded in 1670 by Prince Rupert to promote the fur trade round the shores of Hudson Bay, in an area vaguely defined as Prince Rupert's Land. Gradually the Company extended its interests and its traders pushed westwards to the Rockies, and much early exploration was due to them. The trading posts were important links in the spread of the white man's influence. The story of the H.B.C. is a romance in itself.

*Hudson Bay blanket*. Originally made for the servants of 'The Company', this blanket soon became an article of trade on account of its excellent qualities; to say 'Hudson Bay blanket' is equivalent to saying 'Rolls-Royce'.

*husky*. The Eskimo sledge-dog; a semi-wild animal of mixed breed, but of great endurance.

*Indian*. Grey Owl rightly objected to the term 'Red Indian'. He said it was 'too suggestive of the dime novel and blood-and-thunder literature'. The correct term is 'North-American Indian'. Grey Owl had a high opinion of the knowledge of Indian life and customs shown in Longfellow's *Hiawatha*, and he recognised that Fenimore Cooper 'must have done some travelling with Indians'. The North-American Indians, before the white man came, lived in tribes; each tribe had a hunting area large enough to allow for wandering in search of game. They were nomadic and lived in wigwams, or teepees, which could be moved easily. This life made the men experts in woodcraft and backwoodsmanship, and they have never had their equals. With the coming of the white man, the numbers of Indians decreased through the introduction of new diseases, the sale of spirits, etc. To-day there are probably not more than 100,000 pure-bred Indians in the whole of North America. Some of the deterioration has been arrested by the formation of Indian Reservations, areas where the Indians can live their own lives and maintain their native customs. It is interesting to note that Indian blood—and there has been much intermarrying—is not regarded with the same distaste as black (slave) blood; indeed, many notable men in the United States and in Canada have Indian blood in their veins.

*Indian Summer*. A period of fine, mild weather during late autumn.

*larrigan.* An oil-tanned moccasin of heavy leather, sometimes having a hard sole.

*Mississauga.* A river running from the north into the North Channel of Lake Huron. Its mouth is about seventy miles east of Sault Ste. Marie.

*moccasins.* Soft shoes made of moose-hide or inferior skin. There is no hard sole, and consequently they are ideal for woods travel, as the wearer can feel the ground under his feet and so avoid making alarming noises, such as treading on sticks, etc.

*moose.* The elk of North America and some parts of Northern Europe and Asia. Distinguished by its overhanging upper lip, and, in the male, by the wide-spread palmated antlers.

*muskeg.* Swampy ground.

*Ojibway.* An Indian tribe of Algonquin stock, and sometimes known by that name. They formerly hunted over lands on the north of Lakes Huron and Superior. Grey Owl was adopted by the Ojibways, who gave him his name Wa-Sha-Quon-Asin, 'he who walks by night'. He wrote: 'Half-breed trapper I am, and far more closely identified with the Ojibway Indians than any other people. I want the Ojibways to get their share of any credit that may accrue. I am their man. They taught me much.'

*pan.* The fan-shaped spread of the moose-antler.

*peltry.* Fur.

*portage.* A part of the trail where it is impossible to go by water; all gear must be carried overland to the next navigable stretch. Portages are divided into sections called 'stages', about six or eight minutes apart, that being the length of time experience shows a man can carry a big load without fatigue. He recuperates on the way back for the next load. This is an Indian system, and it has proved better to work in this fashion than by taking smaller loads right through.

*Prince Albert.* A town of some 12,000 inhabitants on the Saskatchewan River. To the north of it lies the Prince Albert National Park, where Grey Owl had his beaver lodge. There are a number of these National Parks in Canada; each is of considerable size, and remains a natural preservation of forest and lake; the public can use them for holidays, but not for hunting.

*reservation,* or reserve. *See* above, 'Indian'.

*runway*. A slope made for greater ease down to the shores of a lake, etc.

*Saskatchewan*. The central province of the prairie region of Canada.

*shingle*. A wooden roof-tile.

*snowshoe*. The Canadian snowshoe is so designed that its broad surface prevents the foot sinking into the snow. It is 3 to 5 ft. long, and 1 to 2 ft. wide. The largest are used by the man who goes ahead to break the trail. The snowshoe is roughly pear-shaped. The frame is made of tough wood, and a network of rawhide thongs (*babiche*) is interlaced between, rather like a tennis racket. There are two loops (*bridles*) into which the toes fit, while the heels are left free. The snowshoe lifts in front only and so crunches down the snow.

*squaw*. Indian woman.

*Temagami*. A lake in the Temagami Forest Reserve of Ontario; the Ottawa River is near.

*teepee*. Conical-shaped tent of skins or birch bark supported by poles.

*tump-line*. Two 10-ft. leather thongs attached to a broad band, which goes over the forehead; the thongs are fastened round the load, and the weight is thus partly taken by the head-band; especially useful in going uphill.

*voyageur*. A man employed by traders to carry goods from place to place. Used generally of Canadian canoe-men. A reminder of the days when Canada was French.

*whiskey-jack*. Common grey jay of Canada; also known as the camp-bird.

*wigwam*. General term for any Indian lodge, cabin or shelter.

www.ingramcontent.com/pod-product-compliance
Ingram Content Group UK Ltd.
Pitfield, Milton Keynes, MK11 3LW, UK
UKHW042146280225
455719UK00001B/150